KU-163-770

Contents

The Politics of Human Rights

WITHDRAWN

Human Security in the Global Economy

Series editor: Professor Caroline Thomas (Southampton University)

Also available

Global Governance, Development and Human Society
The Challenge of Poverty and Inequality
Caroline Thomas

The Politics of Human Rights
A Global Perspective

Tony Evans

Pluto  Press

LONDON • STERLING, VIRGINIA

First published 2001 by Pluto Press
345 Archway Road, London N6 5AA
and 22883 Quicksilver Drive,
Sterling, VA 20166–2012, USA

www.plutobooks.com

British Library Cataloguing in Publication Data
A catalogue record for this book is available from the British Library

Library of Congress Cataloging in Publication Data
Evans, Tony, 1944–
    The politics of human rights : a global perspective / Tony Evans.
      p. cm.— (Human security in the global economy)
    ISBN 0–7453–1457–0
    1. Human rights. 2. Globalization. I. Title. II. Series.

 JC571 .E853 2001
323—dc21
                                                              00–057430

ISBN 0 7453 1457 0 hardback
ISBN 0 7453 1452 X paperback

10   09   08   07   06   05   04   03   02   01
10   9   8   7   6   5   4   3   2   1

Designed and produced for Pluto Press by
Chase Publishing Services, Fortescue, Sidmouth EX10 9QG
Typeset from disk by Stanford DTP Services, Northampton
Printed in the European Union by Antony Rowe, Chippenham, England

Globalization and the Study of Universal Human Rights

The general theme of this series is human security, defined as something more than the conventional concept of military security that has dominated the literature on international relations for so long. Following the United Nations Development Programme's (UNDP) definition, human security refers to 'safety from the constant threats of hunger, disease, crime and repression' and 'protection from sudden and hurtful disruptions to the patterns of our daily lives – whether in the home, in our jobs, in our communities or in our environment'. Human security is not therefore only to do with cataclysmic political and international events, but with 'job security, income security, health security, environmental security ... [and] ... security from crime' (UNDP 1994). The UNDP confirmed this approach to human security in its tenth annual *Human Development Report*, which argues that security is concerned with 'widening the range of people's choices' and the means by which 'people can exercise their choices safely and freely' (UNDP 1999: 36). Accordingly, the purpose of human security is to provide the conditions for people to exercise and expand their choices, capabilities and opportunities free of insecurity, so that they may build a future for themselves and their children (Salih 1998). Whereas military security is concerned with external threats to the state, human security takes a more people-centred focus, particularly the need to create the necessary economic, social and political conditions for people to lead a dignified life. While in the past it may have seemed possible to achieve these conditions largely within the domestic political arena, today, under conditions of globalization, which many argue is placing severe constraints on state authority, achieving human security demands action at the global level (Cox 1994; Gill 1996; Panitch 1995).

Human security is therefore broader than the tradition that understands political community through the language of the territorial state, sovereignty and strategic studies, which stresses the importance of defence, the military and interstate conflict. Instead, those with an interest in human security point to

1

important features of the state and the interstate system that represent barriers to achieving the conditions for leading a dignified life within the emerging global order. For traditionalists, the state remains the central participant in finding solutions to the new threats presented by globalization, even though the causes of these threats are located in new forms of social, political and economic transnational relations, for which a state-centric analysis fails to account. The criticism of the traditional approach to security is that it leads to conservative solutions, more concerned with sustaining the *status quo* than with seriously engaging in the challenges that globalization presents (Walker 1990).

This definitional shift in the security debate is not, therefore, an isolated development within the social science disciplines of international relations and politics, which like all other disciplines are occasionally subject to capricious new fads and fashions. Instead, it should be seen as a consequence of important changes to the global order, away from an international order of states towards an order best captured by the term 'globalization'. This term, which has pervaded academic and popular debate since the end of the 1980s, has stimulated interest in developing a new language that reflects the emerging global order, as evidenced by terms like 'global environmental change', 'global civil society', 'global gendered equality' and 'global development' as measured by the UNDP's Human Development Index. Part of this process includes redefining and reconfiguring old concepts to distinguish them from the past era. Some scholars have argued that the emergence of a new language offers a clear indication that 'something important is unfolding' in any given historic period, for example, that moment which coincided with the emergence of the territorial state as the norm for organizing social relations during the eighteenth century (Scholte 1996). The creation and development of a new language is not, therefore, simply a cosmetic affair, but an attempt to describe, explain and critique a new social order that cannot be grasped by the language and concepts of the past.

Globalization and Human Security

Given that the concept of human security is mediated through the processes and practices of globalization, some brief account of the character of globalization is necessary. There are, of course, many disagreements on the exact nature of globalization, not only across disciplines but within disciplines also (Spybey 1996). However, most theories of globalization begin by broadly accepting that we are witnessing a significant shift in the spatial reach of networks of social relations, which are reflected in the growth of transcontinental, interregional and global relations. Globalization is understood as an historical process that both 'stretches' and 'deepens' transnational patterns of economic, political, military, technological and ecological interactions. 'Stretching' social relations suggests that events, decisions and activities in one part of the world often have an immediate impact on the economic, social and political well-being of individuals and communities in distant locations. This is distinguished from the 'deepening' of social relations, which suggests that patterns of interaction and interconnectedness are achieving both greater density and intensity (McGrew 1992; Held & McGrew 1999). In the words of Anthony Giddens, although 'everyone has a local life, phenomenal worlds for the most part are truly global' (Giddens 1990: 187). The existence of physical, symbolic and normative infrastructures mediates this 'stretching' and 'deepening', for example, systems of air transportation, English as the language of business and science, and images of 'one world', as expressed in the debates on universal human rights and the environment. These infrastructures are themselves associated with the development and spread of new technology, which influences the scale of globalization and circumscribes social interactions (Buzan et al. 1993).

However, individuals, households and communities are differentially enmeshed in the processes and practices of globalization such that control over, and the impact of, these processes vary enormously both between as well as within societies. This differential reach and impact reflects structural asymmetries in the geometry of global power relations. Patterns of hierarchy and stratification mediate access to sites of power while the consequences of globalization are unevenly experienced. For example, the fact that the majority of the world's trade is between Organization for Economic Cooperation and Development (OECD) countries offers testimony to long-standing historical patterns of hierarchy and stratification in the global trading order (Taylor & Thomas 1999). Similarly, the dominant conception of human rights, which gives greater emphasis to civil and political rights rather than economic and social rights, prioritizes the interests of those closest to the processes of economic globalization rather than those on the periphery.

Like many other aspects of human security, efforts to protect universal human rights are not immune from the impacts of globalization. While some studies have attempted to recontextualize human rights as an important aspect of globalization, most, if not all, adopt a neoliberal approach, which tacitly assumes that globalization presents new opportunities for strengthening human security (e.g. Donnelly 1993). Neoliberals tend toward a view of globalization that projects a vision of inexorable progress towards ever increasing levels of 'moral integration', which parallels processes of economic integration, as normative and moral aspirations converge (Donnelly 1989: 211–13). According to neoliberals, these processes provide the context for the emergence of a global civil society, which will, in time, empower the global citizen in the struggle to claim universal human rights and the values associated with those rights. Neoliberals acknowledge that while the past era saw the development of legal standards for universal human rights, in the form of international law that reflects the timeless universalism of rights claims, implementation was inhibited by the principles on which the international system of states was built, including sovereignty, non-intervention and domestic jurisdiction (Cassese 1990). Today, so the argument continues, the conditions of globalization provide an opportunity to develop new forms of 'humane governance', including new and more effective ways of securing universal human rights (Clark 1999: 129).

Critics of neoliberal optimism are less sanguine. First, critics accuse neoliberals of a myopic vision of globalization, which stresses present and future benefits but remains blind to current, potential and future costs. These criticisms argue that the forms of global finance, capital accumulation and consumption associated with globalization are supported by new social, economic and political structures that are no less prone to processes of inclusion and exclusion than in previous periods. Second, critics point out that the institutions on which neoliberals place so much hope for securing human rights, including international law, may well be less effective under conditions of globalization because these institutions reflect the statist logic of the previous era, rather than those of the future (Evans & Hancock 1998). If under conditions of globalization the authority of the state diminished, then international law, the law that governs relations between states, has less potential in regulating the practices of non-state transterritorial actors. Third, critics argue that it is demonstrably over-optimistic to claim that wide agreement has been reached concerning the nature and substance of universal human rights, as can be seen in the recent debates over 'Asian values' and the invisibility of women in the human rights debate (Pasha & Blaney 1998; Tang 1995; Peterson & Parisi 1998). Finally, critics argue that the uneven consequences of globalization suggest that economic and moral integration is not indicative of the emergence of a single, globally accepted moral code. Rather than signalling the 'end of history' (Fukuyama 1989), critics argue, neoliberal observations about processes of global integration suggest the emergence of particular forms of class formation and new hierarchies of knowledge and power (van de Pijl 1998). Neoliberal assertions about the prospects for human rights are therefore little more than a reflection of particular class interests, not an all-embracing global phenomenon that will eventually bring human rights protection to all people, expressed cogently by Scholte:

> ... liberal globalists of the late twentieth century readily fall prey to a naïve optimism, sometimes bordering on the euphoric, that modernity will, almost as a matter of historical inevitability, yield a universal, homogeneous, egalitarian, prosperous and communitarian world society. Yet in practice, globalization has often perpetuated (and in some instances increased) poverty, violence, ecological degradation, estrangement and anomie. [Furthermore], liberal accounts of globalization lack a critical examination of their own terms and the social structures that this mind-set bolsters. Tacitly if not explicitly, liberal orthodoxy treats the market, electoral democracy, growth, national solidarity and scientific reason as timeless virtues with universal applicability. This discourse effectively rules out the possibility that capitalism, individualism, industrialism, consumerism, the nationality principle and rationalism might be causes rather than cures for global problems. (Scholte 1996: 51)

This more pessimistic, critical view of the future of human rights focuses upon the negative aspects of globalization, including mass migrations, refugees, famine, violence, environmental degradation, cultural dissolution and structural deprivation. Pessimists argue that far from strengthening human rights, the practices of globalization may not lead to greater human emancipation, but rather to new forms of repression. For the pessimists, '[t]here is no obvious or unambiguous, let alone, necessary, connection between globalization and freedom' (Scholte 1996: 52). If the project of universal human rights can be further promoted within the context of globalization, then according to the pessimists, we must begin by unmasking the weaknesses and inadequacies of the neoliberal approach so that our hopes are not thwarted and our energies dissipated by undertaking actions that lead to inevitable failure.

This book follows the critical and pessimistic path by attempting to expose some of the more extravagant claims for human rights in the age of globalization. As suggested above, the critical and pessimistic path should be seen as offering an opportunity to contribute to social, economic and political change that will make a lasting contribution to human security and human rights. Given the current configuration of forms of state, global institutions and world order (Cox 1981), the prospect for effecting such changes is severely limited. However, the new social formations that go under the rubric of globalization are not natural phenomena, contrary to the assumptions of some academics and practitioners (see Chapter 6). Instead, these social formations emerge in complex processes to do with the social construction of knowledge and the practical outcomes that follow from particular types of knowledge. The human rights debate is made more complex in this task because, traditionally, it borrows from three overlapping branches of knowledge, a practice that often confuses as much as it clarifies. The aim of this book is to focus on the politics of human rights, as distinguished from the philosophy of rights or human rights law.

Philosophy, Law and the Politics of Universal Human Rights

The disjuncture between the rhetoric and practice of universal human rights presents one of the central puzzles of contemporary global politics, a puzzle that even the most casual observer cannot fail to note. While national and international political leaders, with few exceptions, are quick to endorse the principles of universal human rights, and even quicker to denounce others who violate them, the reports of non-governmental organizations (NGOs) continue to expose the gap between words and action. Similarly, in legal and academic circles, it is common to see claims of 'revolutionary' or 'amazing' progress in the field of human rights during the last fifty years (Opsahl 1989: 33), ignoring the inconvenient facts of widespread torture, genocide, structural economic deprivation, disappearances, ethnic cleansing, political prisoners and the suppression of trade unions and democracy movements. Consequently, human rights engender simultaneous feelings of optimism and pessimism: optimism because the rhetoric suggests that human rights are now a cardinal concern that informs the decisions of all political leaders, and pessimism because the expanding global communications system exposes us to vivid images of gross human rights violations almost daily.

One of the central reasons for the tensions between feelings of optimism and pessimism can be found in the nature of what Vincent called 'human rights talk' (Vincent 1986), which is not a singular debate but three overlapping discourses within the same debate, each with its own language, concepts and normative aims. These three discourses are the philosophical, the legal and the political.

The philosophy of rights is an abstract discourse. Historically, it has been concerned with discovering the foundations upon which legitimate claims for universal human rights might be justified and sustained. Although the history of Western philosophical thought has long appealed to various interpretations of natural law theory to provide this foundation, other avenues have also been investigated, including self-evidence, human needs and the existence of a deity (Marks 1998). More recently, a postmodernist turn in philosophy has gained some ground, arguing that all attempts to find a secure foundation for human rights are futile (Rorty 1993). While there is a growing interest in this anti-foundational approach, the foundationalist project continues to inform the dominant themes of much 'human rights talk' today. A second broad area of philosophical investigation attempts to describe a future moral order in which human rights might be realized. Speculation within this line of enquiry often focuses upon new forms of citizenship, justice and democracy that, if adopted, will resolve the problems associated with globalization, interdependence and changes in the world order (Linklater 1998).

Given the abstract, moral nature of the philosophy of rights discourse, and the reality of continuous reports of starvation, genocide and torture, it is little wonder that our feelings oscillate between optimism and pessimism. This is not an argument for abandoning the discourse on the philosophy of rights, as Robinson has pointed out (Robinson 1998: 60). However, it is an argument for attempting to raise our awareness of the social, economic and political contexts in which human rights might be secured and upon which the new utopia might be built. The starting point for investigating the current and future development of human rights should not therefore be restricted to abstract thought and reason. Instead, as Antonio Gramsci has pointed out, it should begin by noting the real activities found in global society, including those practices that generate human rights violations, for example, the human rights consequences of trade which are discussed later. Since there is an ethical dimension to all social, economic and political action, the serious contradictions we observe between the theory and practice of human rights raises questions about how we should understand and evaluate the achievements of the philosophical discourse (Gramsci 1996: 326).

In contrast to the philosophical discourse on universal human rights, the legal discourse focuses upon a large body of international law. At the centre of this discourse is the Universal Declaration of Human Rights and the two major covenants, one on civil and political rights and the other on economic, social and cultural rights. The legal discourse can also be divided into two broad areas. The first involves disagreements over the nature and status of international law in a world where sovereignty, non-intervention and domestic jurisdiction remain the guiding principles (Evans & Hancock 1998). It is therefore concerned with detecting qualitative changes in world order, which in the case of human rights law are said to have transformed the principles of international law to a system of law more appropriately labelled 'transnational law' (Cassese 1990). Importantly, international lawyers and legal scholars are often concerned to demonstrate that, under the international law on human rights, states cannot any longer, as a matter of fact, withdraw behind the protective shield of sovereignty as a means of avoiding human rights obligations. While some international lawyers might argue that this approach 'impedes the application of basic international legal doctrine to human rights law, impedes its conceptual and academic development and obscures conflicts between the two' (Chinkin 1998: 106), the attempt to separate human rights law from other types of international law attracts considerable attention, particularly under conditions of globalization.

The second broad focus for international law concerns questions to do with the internal elegance of the law, its coherence, extent and meaning, which the application of legal reason discovers (Young 1989). Lawyers and academics who attempt to examine a particular violation or deprivation of a human right commonly resort to an extensive analysis of covenants, declarations, constitutions and General Assembly resolutions, an approach that excludes consideration of actual behaviour in its particular social and political context. Following this approach often leads to confusion between the obligations articulated in international law and the political and social norms that condition social behaviour. The tendency to confuse political and social norms with international legal norms may inspire a sense of progress in those who seek solutions to the pressing problems surrounding the protection of human rights, but it also risks offering hope when none is justified.

The legal discourse provides the most visible sign of human rights activity. However, critics argue that visibility and weight of paper are not necessarily attributes of efficacy. Too often the human rights literature makes implicit assumptions about the relationship between international law and the protection of human rights, which is never clearly articulated. This offers the false impression that the protection of human rights can be guaranteed provided we exercise diligence and reason when drafting and interpreting international law, although it is rare to find any justification for this assumption. If Johan Galtung's contention is true that most violations of human rights owe more to current economic and political structures than to the evil side of human nature, then assumptions about legal efficacy are questionable (Galtung 1994). The claim that the legal discourse on human rights is pitched within the realm of 'wishful thinking', together with the observation that a narrow concern to discover the 'true' meaning of internationally agreed human rights treaties or the legitimate authority invested in legally constituted organs of government, obscures and confuses rather than enlightens and clarifies, is therefore apposite (Vincent 1986; Barkun 1968).

The political discourse on human rights attempts to contextualize the philosophical and legal discourses. It is concerned with raising questions to do with why human rights have emerged as a significant issue in the post-Second World War order and why some sets of rights receive greater attention than others. In common with all political questions, the political discourse on human rights pays special attention to power relationships (Stammers 1993, 1995; Evans 1996), including those associated with social and economic power. While law and philosophy are often discussed within the literature on the politics of rights, this is most often concerned with asking questions about dominant forms of legal and philosophical reasoning and the interests served by the dominant conceptualization of human rights. Following the end of the Cold War, and in the age of globalization, the political discourse is also concerned with understanding the place of human rights in a changing world order, where the power of the state is often eclipsed by that of international organizations, transnational corporations and financial institutions.

The literature on the politics of rights is perhaps the least developed of the three discourses that constitute 'human rights talk'. The reasons for this are complex but can be expressed briefly in two points. First, while many see the philosophy of rights as the application of reason, and international law as a neutral code for protecting human rights, they understand politics as neither neutral nor subject to reason. Instead, within 'human rights talk' politics is understood as a value-laden, ideological discourse concerned with power and interests, which offers cause for distracting conflicts that do not help to promote human rights. Second, even if it were possible to claim a close relationship between the norms of the three discourses at the domestic level, this claim is doubtful at the international or global level. Although political leaders and academics often assert the existence of a global society, which is defined by a generally accepted set of norms, including the norms of universal human rights, it remains contestable whether such a society has so far emerged (Pasha & Blaney 1998). For human rights, where the historic contribution of reason (philosophy) and neutrality (law) are widely recognized, politics is often seen as an impediment to achieving the goal of a single global community. This is not to argue that all lawyers and all philosophers ignore the political context of rights but that the political fits uneasily with reason, neutrality and arguments associated with universal values. Politics has therefore played the lesser role in 'human rights talk', despite its pivotal role in both the creation and development of the post-Second World War human rights regime (Evans 1996).

One further danger should be mentioned concerning the habit of conflating legal, philosophical and political norms. This habit allows the terms, concepts and language of the three discourses to be used interchangeably, a phenomenon that is often seen in the academic literature, the media and the utterances of political leaders. Since the meanings attached to language often vary among the three discourses, the scope for creating confusion is immense (Evans 1996: 23–2). Following from this is the danger of circularity, where a political question is given a legal answer, which in turn is deflected by a philosophical objection that raises a further political question. This is not a reason for maintaining rigid boundaries to the three discourses, for such a path would run against the current trend to weaken the existing division between the various disciplines that are the social and political sciences. However, an awareness of these dangers is an essential element in any attempt to understand the place of universal human rights in the emerging global order.

It is the tripartite nature of human rights talk that adds to simultaneous feelings of optimism and pessimism. The abstract, moral, utopian approach of philosophy, which allows us to glimpse a better future, fills us with hope, while the empirical, neutral, norm-driven approaches of international law reassure us that international society has taken firm action on human rights. Together these two discourses conspire to marginalize the political discourse, and thus exclude consideration of prevailing economic, social and political structures and practices that support particular interests while sustaining the conditions for continued human rights violations. The aim of this book is to investigate some aspects of the political discourse more thoroughly and, through focusing on the politics of rights, to understand the ambiguous nature of the project at the beginning of the twenty-first century.

The Structure of the Book

This book takes a critical and pessimistic view of the development of universal human rights in its current guise. The arguments presented in the following chapters should not be taken as a rejection of the idea of universal human rights. On the contrary, as the conditions of globalization increasingly touch the lives of all people, there is an even greater need to establish mechanisms that offer greater human security. This is particularly urgent if we take account of the distinction often made in globalization theory between government and governance. With this in mind, the following chapters attempt to expose some of the contradictions, weaknesses and misunderstandings in the current theory and practice of human rights. At the heart of the arguments presented here is the failure of current theory and practice to take proper and full account of globalization as the new context in which universal human rights must be embedded. Theorists and practitioners who fail to gain an insight into the social, political and economic dimensions of globalization, and continue to offer analysis and solutions that refer to a past era, participate in perpetuating the myth of great progress in the field of human rights, where no such claim is justified.

The following chapters expand on the idea of the politics of human rights. The five areas selected as the focus of these chapters do not, of course, represent the full spectrum of the politics of rights. Many other issues might have been included, for example, the possibility of environmental rights and feminist critiques of the human rights project. Furthermore, the critical thrust of these chapters is intended to raise questions rather than offer solutions. The intention is to highlight the politics of rights in a way that provokes reflection and further analysis before beginning the task of reformulating the human rights project. I have also tried to make each chapter as self-contained as possible, so that the reader can choose their own point of entry. This has inevitably lead to some overlap between the chapters, particularly when dealing with the literature on globalization. However, where this does occur, it has been kept to a minimum and, where appropriate, is indicated in the text.

The first chapter begins with a brief overview of the role of power before moving to examine the politics of the current human rights regime within the institutions of the United Nations Organization. This is set within the context of the global political economy and the emergence of the United States as the new global hegemon. The argument presented here is that the birth of the human rights regime cannot be understood solely as a response to the horrors of Nazism, as is often claimed. While the shock of the concentration camps and the revelations of the Holocaust certainly played a part, a further insight is gained by looking at the postwar regime as a response to international and domestic economic interests. Although many socialist and less developed countries resisted these interests, the character of the regime was set during the early years following the creation of the Commission for Human Rights. Following the collapse of the Cold War, and the decline in influence of the socialist states, an understanding of universal human rights that serve particular interests has achieved even greater legitimacy than in the past. In short, economic and social rights that could have empowered the poor in their fight against exploitation and exclusion, now take second place to civil and political rights, or those rights that support freedom in the private sphere of economic interests.

The second chapter reassesses the place of universal human rights in the age of globalization. The discussion is set within the context of sharp disagreements on the nature of the post-Cold War world order, which add complexity to understanding the prospects for human rights. Important here is the debate over the role of the state under conditions of globalization and the realistic prospects for the state to secure human rights for its citizens. Central to this discussion is an examination of the role of international law in a changing world.

A third chapter focuses on the political economy of human rights, specifically the relationship between free trade and human rights. It examines the traditional liberal view of free trade and human rights before looking at some criticisms levelled against this view. It then goes on to suggest that the arguments for protecting global economic interests in the name of promoting human rights do not stand up to scrutiny. Following this discussion, the chapter then moves to look at the role of free trade under conditions of globalization, the priority given to trade and the marginalization of rights issues when trade interests prevail. The chapter concludes with some examples of trade-related human rights violations.

Chapter 4 looks at the assumption that human rights and democracy are symbiotic. It argues that this assumption is less secure than it appears at first sight, particularly when the imperative of economic growth and development is pressing. The chapter continues by arguing that some states are democratic only in as far as they possess the formal institutions of democracy, as opposed to those social institutions that support democratic outcomes, including the protection of human rights. It then goes on to look at the politics of the democracy–human rights nexus, as it is promoted in many quarters and concludes that the needs of the global economy are once again at the centre of any explanation.

Chapter 5 discusses the claim that globalization will eventually see the development of the international citizen, international civil society and the necessary conditions for improved promotion of universal human rights. This is done by looking at the difficulties of conceptualizing the international citizen in a world that has witnessed the transformation of both state authority and the relationship between civil society and citizenship. The chapter goes on to question ideas of international citizenship, international civil society and the idea of tolerance. The conclusion suggests that these concepts lend legitimacy to global practices that support particular interests already fully integrated into the global economy, rather than the interests of those whose human rights and human security are in need of protection.

Finally, some of the themes of the book are brought together in a conclusion.

CHAPTER 1

The Politics of Universal Human Rights

This chapter looks in more detail at the politics of universal human rights, as distinct from the philosophy of rights or international human rights law. It begins with an examination of the relationship between power and the concept of universal human rights. This suggests that the current conception of human rights, like all dominant conceptions of rights, is the outcome of a political struggle aimed at achieving moral legitimacy. This is followed by a section that looks at the rise of human rights in the post-Second World War order and, more particularly, the role of the United States in placing human rights on the political agenda. A further section looks at the socialist and less developed countries' challenge to the US's conception of universal human rights. The clash of ideologies, which was at the core of all Cold War struggles, meant that the United States sought to withdraw its support for the global human rights regime. Instead, the US used its considerable political and economic power to promote a particular conception of human rights that sought to legitimate its own interests and those of capital. A penultimate section suggests that the post-Cold War order, which some suggest marks the end of the contemporary struggle over the concept of human rights, will not provide a more propitious context for rights than in the past. Finally, some brief remarks will be made about the future of universal human rights, in preparation for the following chapters.

Human Rights as Politics

The creation of the United Nations placed universal human rights at the centre of global politics. Human rights are mentioned in the UN Charter seven times, including Article 68, which calls for the creation of the Commission on Human Rights. The Commission completed the final draft of the Universal Declaration of Human Rights (UDHR) during its first eighteen months of deliberations, a remarkable achievement, rarely matched before or since, for reaching any international agreement. That the UDHR remains the single, most important statement of human rights norms, more than fifty years later, places this achievement into even sharper perspective. In the following decades the Commission drafted a series of legally binding treaties, the most important of which are the International Covenant on Civil and Political Rights (ICCPR) and the International Covenant on Economic, Social and Cultural Rights (ICESCR). Other legally binding instruments include the Convention on the Prevention and Punishment of the Crime of Genocide (Genocide Convention), the Convention Against Torture and Other Cruel, Inhuman or Degrading Treatments or Punishments (Torture Convention) and the Convention on the Elimination of All Forms of Discrimination Against Women (CEDAW). The Commission also put in place procedures for implementing the rights set out in these treaties, including monitoring, periodic reports and arbitration. The Americas, Africa and Europe have also established regional human rights regimes with varying degrees of effectiveness.

Yet, despite all this activity, violations of human rights are almost a commonplace. Newspapers and other news media are filled with graphic reports and images of human rights violations, describing acts widely acknowledged as unlawful under international law. The disjuncture between the formal norms set out under international law and the normal practices of governments, transnational corporations, international financial institutions, the military and the police suggest two possibilities. The first, which human rights scholars widely accept, is that the international community has not matched its enthusiasm for setting human rights standards with a similar enthusiasm for creating the necessary machinery to implement those standards. Although the Commission on Human Rights has developed monitoring procedures and advisory programmes for implementing state obligations under international law, commentators generally acknowledge that these are weak. The problem of how to secure universal values in an international system of sovereign states, defined by the principles of domestic jurisdiction and non-intervention, remains at the centre of this observation. The second possibility concerns an approach to securing human rights that emphasizes post-violation redress, rather than an alternative approach that looks at the causes of violations and the means of prevention. This approach is reflected in the recent creation of an International Criminal Court and the courts set up to try perpetrators of human rights crimes in Rwanda and the former Yugoslavia. That the causes of many violations might be found in the structures of the global political economy, and the interests that these structures support, may offer some insight into why redress is favoured over structural reform. This second reason for the failure to provide adequate protection for human rights offers a central theme throughout this book.

As discussed in the Introduction, the theory and practice of human rights is generally conducted in the language of legal and philosophical reason, which focuses upon international law, methods of implementation and the source, justification and meaning of rights. If political questions concerning power and interest are considered at all, commentators usually view them within a realist or international society conception of global politics, which stresses the principles of sovereignty, domestic jurisdiction and non-intervention in the affairs of legitimate states (Kennan 1985; Vincent 1986). In this construction of the human rights debate, the legal, philosophical and political discourses that constitute 'human rights talk' adopt a liberal framework (Vincent 1986), leaving little room for alternative conceptions or interpretations that might raise challenging questions about current theory and practice. What legitimating role do human rights play in the current global order? Do all individuals and groups benefit from the dominant conception of universal human rights? Why do powerful Western liberal democracies so vigorously defend their particular conception of human rights? What role does the global political economy play in securing or denying access to the means for protecting human rights? Is international law the most effective way of promoting all human rights? Can we sustain the claim that human rights and democracy are two sides of the same coin, as many Western commentators assume? What is the future of human rights in the age of globalization? Although some authors have attempted to look at these questions in recent times, the dominant epistemology of human rights does not encourage such enquiry.

The convention of understanding 'progress' in the field of human rights by reference to law, including the creation of international institutions, reflects a widely held assumption that reason and rationality have triumphed over politics. These assumptions are often reflected in the assertion that the creation of the UDHR represents a symbolic moment of 'arrival', when the reason of rights finally prevailed, following two hundred years of struggle (Raphael 1967). At the end of the Cold War, which for some marks the 'end of history' (Fukuyama 1989), all that is left for the human rights debate are technical issues to do with improving implementational procedures and drafting new international laws that clarify already legitimated and universally accepted norms. If politics has any further role, it is confined to disagreements over these technical issues, which are themselves conditioned by the 'givens' of the existing, liberal world order. Power and interests are no longer part of the struggle for human rights. Consequently, with 'depressing regularity', those engaged in the theory and practice of human rights are prone to offering us exhortations of optimism and hope, which are 'almost always expressed in the passive voice to increase its apparent authority' (Watson 1979). What such an approach indicates is that the author's argument is based more upon his or her perceptions of human nature, including a vision of how human beings 'ought' to treat one another, rather than the theory and practice of the current human rights regime.

For the critical reader, or simply the puzzled observer, the optimism found in the literature cannot be reconciled with the overwhelming evidence of human rights violations. What this situation reveals is the failure to take full account of the social and political construction of rights, the particular configuration of world order in which the current human rights regime operates and the interests that the current regime sustains. Given the political context of both the French and American revolutions, which are widely understood as seminal moments in the modern human rights movement, this seems a strange omission. These revolutions represent the climax of the struggle to overthrow an old social order and legitimate the new. They are revolutions in the sense that they sought a radical transformation of the accepted principles of social organization, rather than a mere seizure of power within the existing order. Thus, the principles of the new order – the people as sovereign, the authority of the civil adminis-tration and the rights of the citizen – replaced the principles of the old order – the divine right of kings, the authority of the Church and a duty to obey the monarch. Following the success of these revolutions, the old order, which for centuries provided the social context for political and economic action, was revealed as oppressive and tyrannical and the new as offering the conditions for human dignity, personal freedom and a future without fear.

From these historic events we can conclude that moral claims are closely linked to processes associated with the legitimation of interests. In other words, 'ideas and practices concerning human rights are *created* by people in particular historical, social and economic circumstances' (Stammers 1995: 488, original emphasis). The regimes that emerged from the French and American revolutions sought to legitimate their authority through the new language of natural law and human rights, which suggested an inclusive harmony of interests. The separation of private and economic life from public and political life, which is central to natural rights, was presented as a moral imperative in the interests of all the people, not the outcome of new power rela-tionships that served the interests of particular groups. Although natural rights did not reveal 'any universal truths about the rela-tionship between individuals, society and the state' (Stammers 1993: 74), it provided a moral justification for overthrowing the old order and replacing it with one that legitimated the interests of the dominant group in the new. As Issa Shivji has argued, human rights 'mirror the struggles and concerns of the dominant groups in society at a particular time as these groups organize and reorganize to maintain their position' or to overthrow the existing order (Shivji 1999: 253).

The political discourse on human rights therefore seems to offer two possible views of the role of power. The first suggests 'power to the people' in that human rights offers the oppressed, the excluded and the victims of tyrannical government an opportunity to gain the 'moral high ground' in the struggle for emancipation and freedom. The second sees human rights as 'power over people', expressed in exclusionary practices that deny the full participation of those who fail to support the interests of the dominant group (Evans 1997a). If the contradictions between ideas of freedom and the practice of exclusion are noted at all, the dominant group typically justifies these by arguing either that the excluded do not have the moral capacity to engage fully in decision-making processes or by simply labelling them 'mad' (Hindess 1992; Keeley 1990). Thus, the concept of human rights often supports competing conceptions that give a focus to deeply rooted political struggles. Put another way, the formal, institutionalized and legal practices of human rights reflect and sustain the interests of a dominant group in the existing order, while informal, privately motivated and, on occasion, extralegal action reflects the interest of an alternative order (Stammers 1999). Such a conclusion does, of course, raise questions about the role and status of many non-governmental organizations (NGOs) who seek to promote human rights through formal means. The answers to these questions are not pursued here, but may rely upon understanding NGOs as co-opted organizations that lend further legitimacy to the established order, rather than a radical movement that seeks to challenge that order (Taylor 2001).

Hegemony and Human Rights

The United Nations Charter placed the promotion of human rights at the centre of the post-Second World War order. Given the historic relationship between human rights and interests described above, we have little reason to believe that the postwar order is any different from that of the past: human rights and interests remain inexorably linked. During much of the postwar period, hegemony has referred to the existence of a single dominant state, possessed of the material capabilities and political will to maintain a world order that reflects the hegemon's own interests (Keohane 1984). In this context, the promotion of universal values, like human rights, might seem a distraction, particularly in an order said to be characterized by sovereignty, hegemony and the principles of non-intervention. However, social and political control is not maintained solely through the threat of military coercion, although on occasion the threat and use of force may be necessary, but rather through a system of formal and informal norms and rules that legitimate and shape the actions of weaker states. Recalling the French and American revolutions, at times of radical change in world order, the emergent hegemon seeks to distinguish itself from the past by articulating values that express its moral superiority in the new era.

Explaining this phenomenon requires an examination of the hegemon's need to command obedience to rules that support its own interests without resort to the costly use of force. Recent attempts to explain this phenomenon have drawn upon the work of the Italian Marxist Antonio Gramsci. Gramsci argues that coercion alone cannot guarantee the long-term success of a hegemon, particularly where the resources necessary for coercion do not grow at the same rate as the hegemon's sphere of influence. Instead, the hegemon must foster a consensus around a set of values that support the hegemon's interests. Hegemony is therefore sustained in two ways: first, *externally*, by administering rewards and punishments and, secondly, *internally*, by providing 'intellectual and moral leadership' that shapes the beliefs, wants, opinions and values that reflect the hegemon's interests (Gramsci 1996: 57–8). In Gramsci's conception of hegemony, order is maintained through a 'common social-moral language' that expresses a singular vision of reality, 'informing with its spirit all forms of thought and behaviour' (Femia 1987: 24). The highest form of hegemony is exercised when the hegemon's values are accepted as 'common sense' (Gramsci 1971: 419–25). Expressed more formally, less powerful actors are subject to processes of 'socialization' that bind the ruler and the ruled in a consensual order that legitimates power (Ikenberry & Kupchan 1990). In short, the hegemon exercises control through a combination of might and the legitimation of right.

Gramsci's conception of hegemony offers the prospect of gaining an insight into the postwar politics of rights, including the role of the United States as the new global hegemon. The postwar economic potential of the United States was greater than any other country. US interests held more than seventy per cent of global financial assets and manufacturing output nearly doubled between 1938 and 1946, while other industrialized economies either declined or stagnated (*UN Statistical Yearbook* 1948). To exploit this historic opportunity, the United States sought to establish a new postwar world order safe for American export of goods and capital (Cafruny 1989: 110). Without finding new markets, postwar overproduction promised high unemployment, social unrest and a return to the days of the Depression. Added to this were isolationist calls to withdraw US troops from Europe immediately peace broke out, which, if heeded, would add millions to the ranks of the unemployed. To circumvent these dangers, the United States pursued two broad policies: first, support for postwar reconstruction in Europe and other regions of the world, a policy intended to re-establish markets as quickly as possible; and second, the establishment of a high-profile military presence in selected strategic countries to protect and police those markets.

It was therefore important that the United States did not return to its historic policy of isolationism, which informed its foreign policy during the interwar years (Evans 1996: 51–6; Chomsky 1994: 100–5). Supporting human rights as a universal principle – as a symbol of solidarity related to ideas of universal freedom and *laissez-faire* – offered the potential to resolve some of these problems by mobilizing public support for a new international political and economic order with the United States actively at its centre (Loth 1988).

During the years of war against fascism, wartime leaders saw the idea of human rights as a symbol that inspired the necessary ethos to sustain public support for a prolonged struggle. The call for the universal application of human rights inspired a sense of solidarity. The US Federal Government did not ask Americans to fight merely for a patriotic cause but for the survival of human freedom itself. Fascism not only represented a threat to state security but a threat to the life, liberty and happiness of all people everywhere. The Roosevelt Administration, for example, stressed that to be an American one had to act to protect a set of values that were the very rationale for the creation of the United States itself (Strong 1980). At the core of these values were the ideas of limited government, individual freedom, liberalism and *laissez-faire* economics, which some have argued have their roots in the motivations of the early settlers (Augelli & Murphy 1988). In a speech to the US Congress on 6 January 1941, President Roosevelt articulated these values, an event that is often cited as marking the birth of the modern human rights movement (Roosevelt 1941). In that speech, Roosevelt sketched his blueprint for a new world order founded upon four essential freedoms: freedom of speech, freedom of religion, freedom from fear and freedom from want.

Although at first sight these freedoms appear to go beyond a liberal conception of rights, the freedom from want was not intended to suggest freedom from economic deprivation or a right to social welfare. Instead, freedom from want was defined as an 'economic understanding which will secure for every nation a healthy peacetime life for its inhabitants everywhere in the world' (Roosevelt 1941). Thus, the freedom from want did not suggest that the deprived, the poor and the excluded had a right to claim assistance from those who benefited most from the global economy, but rather that states accepted a duty to remove structural, commercial and cultural barriers between states as those barriers threatened the potential expansion of liberalism on a global scale (Marks 1998). Such an approach to freedom from want remains prevalent today. For example, the economic assistance policies of the international financial institutions, particularly structural adjustment programmes, are aimed at creating the necessary conditions for a strong private sector at the expense of public policy designed to support the poor and excluded (Pugh 2000).

The postwar project for universal human rights therefore provided a vital image in gaining the support of Americans for US entry into the war and, later, an important image in justifying the United States' global role in the postwar order. The Roosevelt Administration argued that Americans had a duty to remain engaged in world politics and to defend the universal human rights of all people everywhere (Hoffman 1977: 9). However, the project to promote universal human rights should also be seen within the context of hegemony and power (Falk 1980). By defining human rights as that set of rights associated with liberalism, the United States sought to project its sphere of influence over a much wider area and to gain access to world markets (Chomsky 1998). As the new economic and moral leader of the emerging postwar order, the United States sought to legitimate its role and thus justify intervention whenever and wherever others failed to act according to the interest of American capital. Crucially, the success of the project rested upon gaining popular international approval for a set of civil and political rights associated with liberalism, or more accurately, with that particular set of rights already enshrined in the Constitution of the United States of America.

The Postwar Development of Human Rights

Richard Falk has pointed to the obvious tension between the need to promote universally accepted values, like human rights, and the exercise of hegemony (Falk 1981). The legitimation of universal values places constraints on all states, even the hegemon. The potential difficulties found in this tension are ameliorated if the hegemon is successful in gaining legitimacy for a set of rights that reflect its own existing social order, beliefs and practices. As early as the Dumbarton Oaks Conversation, which paved the way for the creation of the United Nations, US policy makers found it difficult to sustain a human rights agenda that supported the expansion of American interests. This was for two reasons, one internal and the other external. Internally, isolationist fervour re-emerged in some quarters, bringing with it a fear that the proposed United Nations Organization would develop into a 'World Government', which would enmesh the United States in a set of values that were 'un-American' (Evans 1996; Tananbaum 1988). Externally, as the debate on human rights gained momentum, conservatives came to realize that the rights clearly associated with 'being an American' were not necessarily those that other countries accepted willingly (Evans 1996).

The introduction of New Deal policies in the United States during the 1930s, which increased the role of the federal government in civil rights and welfare issues, had alarmed many conservative groups. These groups argued that the New Deal threatened to erode the constitutional rights of the states incrementally. These fears were further heightened by the racial integration of troops during the war and the growing concern in Washington over segregated education. A report by the Commission on Civil Rights that recommended outlawing certain racist policies also added to conservative fears. Conservatives saw the federal Constitution as the only bulwark against a federal government intent on imposing programmes of civil rights that challenged state laws on segregation, interracial marriage and restrictions on the ownership of property by some racial groups (Kaufman & Whiteman 1988). Eleanor Roosevelt, the chairperson of the Commission of Human Rights during the drafting debate on the Declaration, was warned by one of her Department of State advisers that 'certain elements among the southern contingent and the reactionaries from other parts of the country' would vigorously resist any treaty that might serve either as a basis for federal civil rights legislation or for establishing economic and social rights enforceable under international law (Hendrick, undated).

Domestic resistance to the United States taking a full part in the United Nations or entering into any legally binding agreement on universal human rights took several forms. First, under the Constitution, international treaties are enforceable in all of the states. Ratifying a human rights treaty had the potential of challenging the separate lawmaking powers of the states and overturning existing laws that discriminated on grounds of sex, race, colour, language, property, birth or opinion. The influential American Bar Association argued that a binding human rights treaty would outlaw existing state laws relating to women, miscegenation, and membership of the Communist Party. Second, conservative groups argued that the ratification of any international agreement on human rights would lead to the annulment of existing federal laws on immigration and naturalization, forfeiting the right to determine who should or should not enter the country. In speeches with titles like 'Giving America Away' and 'The Greatest Threat to Our American Heritage', the president of the American Bar Association, F.E. Holman, argued that a human rights treaty threatened to open the floodgates, forcing the United States to accept a 'multitude' of Chinese, Indian and Indonesian people who wanted to leave their own 'already overpopulated countries' (Holman 1952, 1953). Third, conservatives argued that any human rights treaty would empower the federal government to enact new civil rights and social legislation that would not be otherwise enacted (Tananbaum 1988).

At the international level, resistance to the US conception of human rights was also growing. The feeling of solidarity, of being engaged in the 'great adventure' to transform the principles of world politics by placing human rights as its centre, was short-lived (Humphrey 1984). The United States soon discovered that the conception of human rights associated with 'being an American' did not satisfy all countries. While the characteristics of 'being an American' included the virtue of tolerance, such tolerance did not extend to alternative visions of the future, particularly if those visions promoted collective, economic and social rights.

Although the potential for disagreements over the conception of human rights was exposed during the discussions on creating the United Nations, they were not confronted until the Commission on Human Rights convened. The socialist states mounted the early resistance to a liberal conception of human rights. Drawing on Marxist theory, these states argued that the end of the Second World War marked the dawn of a new epoch, which would see a transition from capitalism to socialism. Human rights should therefore reflect the forces of history that would bring a 'new and bright future for the individual in the vast field of social rights' (General Assembly Official Records (GAOR), Czechoslovakia, 3rd session, com. III, 69; Kudryartsev 1986). It followed from this that any durable agreement on human rights should reflect the values of a future world order, not those of the past, including economic and social rights, such as the right to work and social security. According to the socialist countries, those rights developed in the US and Europe during the seventeenth and eighteenth centuries were nothing less than a reactionary attempt to legitimate a set of outmoded, middle-class, bourgeois values that did little for the interests of the poor and excluded. In short, socialist countries argued that their view of human rights was progressive, while that of the West clung conservatively to outmoded ideas and values. Expressed cogently by the Ukrainian representative during the drafting debate for the Declaration, the human rights regime supported by Western countries was the product of minds ignorant of the forces of history, 'directed at the past not the future' (Mannilsky, GAOR, 3rd session).

Less developed countries supported the socialist countries' criticisms of the liberal conception of human rights in three ways. First, the less developed countries argued that the UN Charter had already placed human rights at the centre of the new world order. The UN therefore had a right to take action in defence of human rights, despite the provisions of Article 2(7), which prohibits intervention. Accordingly, any additional international law concerning human rights was likely to obfuscate the principles set out in the Charter and make the protection of human rights more difficult (GAOR, 3rd session, com. III, 43). Second, the less developed countries agreed with the socialist states that economic and social rights should not take second place to civil and political rights. While civil and political rights remained important, their fulfilment could not be divorced from economic and social rights. Third, less developed countries took the principle of self-determination at face value, including permanent sovereignty over natural resources. Such an interpretation of self-determination was unacceptable to Western states, who saw it as a threat to legitimate the nationalization of foreign corporations and the expropriation of capital.

The arguments presented by the socialist and less developed countries only served to strengthen the resolve of conservative and isolationist groups within the United States to press the federal government to recant on the commitment to play a full role in the human rights regime. In particular, conservatives saw the drive to prioritize economic and social rights, or even to grant parity with civil and political rights, as an attempt to ensnare the United States in a complex international and legal system that sought to penetrate, influence and finally bring down the traditional social and political freedoms for which America stood (Tananbaum 1988: Ch. 3). In short, some Americans began to see the effort to promote human rights as a means to achieving what President Eisenhower once referred to as 'socialism by treaty' (Eisenhower 1963: 287). Although the conservative and isolationist lobbies failed to remove all references to economic and social rights in the UDHR, conservatives continued to press the federal government for a reassurance that the United States would never ratify any legally binding international treaty on human rights. Indeed, it can be argued that the UDHR was accepted by the United States only because of its non-legally binding status.

This left the government of the United States with a dilemma. On the one hand, the federal government had invoked human rights as the rationale for engaging in a European war and had raised the expectation that human rights would play a central role in the postwar order. On the other hand, the emergence of competing conceptions of human rights heightened conservative fears about the challenge that human rights presented to existing social and economic values and practices. Furthermore, the federal government was aware of the importance of securing moral leadership in support of the US's new hegemonic role. To add to this complexity, the practical application of the principle of self-determination promised rapid decolonization, increasing the proportion of UN members from less developed countries and, consequently, the creation of a growing majority that sought to challenge the liberal conception of human rights. Although the progress of the Universal Declaration caused the United States some anxiety, the generality of the language and its non-binding legal status presented few threats. However, as the debate turned to the creation of legally binding international law, the United States sought to debase the importance of the formal human rights debate at the UN (Evans 1996). Instead, the United States attempted to use its hegemonic power to assert a conception of human rights that supported its own interests within the postwar political economy.

The examination of the human rights debate as a political discourse offers an insight into the tensions between optimism and pessimism in the literature. Optimists point to the impressive amount of international law generated at the UN, together with the institutions created to monitor and implement human rights, which offers the impression that the world takes human rights seriously. However, one author has likened such optimism to an alien from outer space who, having noted both the number of international treaties and the extent of the ratifications, reports to its home planet that the protection of human rights is one of the great achievements of us earthlings (Schachter 1970). Pessimists, on the other hand, point to continued reports of gross violations of human rights, inconsistences between theory and practice and the cynical use of human rights as a political tool in foreign policy (Chomsky 1998).

For most of the period since the end of the Second World War the formal human rights debate carried out at the UN has lacked the political commitment of a hegemon and has thus 'pirouetted around a missing centre' (Moskovitz 1974: 16). The political programme initiated by the United States, which attempted to withdraw from the formal debate while vigorously promoting a narrow conception of rights that supported US interests, failed to offer any clear leadership. Throughout the years of the Cold War, human rights were treated by both sides as a domain in which to play out the ideological struggle between capitalism and socialism.

Both sides sought to promote their own particular conception of human rights as a way of demonstrating their respective moral superiority and legitimating their respective political systems. As the conception of human rights supported by the socialist states gained support from an increasing number of newly independent countries, the United States promoted human rights through a less formal, political debate, which stressed only those rights that supported American capital and its hegemonic ambitions. In this way, the politics of rights ensured its status as an unfulfilled promise.

The Post-1998 World Order and Human Rights

This final section looks at some of the most important themes to emerge in the human rights debate following the end of the Cold War. Many of these issues are discussed in greater detail in the following chapters but are mentioned here in the context of power, hegemony and rights.

For many commentators, the end of the ideological struggle between East and West promised a new world order that placed humanitarian issues at the heart of international politics. In the early years of the post-Cold War period, the United Nations seemed ready to support intervention whenever and wherever gross violations of human rights occurred. For example, human rights were invoked as a justification for the Gulf War and for intervention in Bosnia, encouraging the view that the new world order would at last enable the United Nations to fulfil its obligations under the Charter. The end of the Cold War was said to mark the beginning of a period where the international community moved on from the agenda of standard setting that dominated the previous four decades, to an agenda concerned with methods for implementing human rights.

However, this optimism was built upon a set of assumptions that continued to reflect old Cold War thinking, rather than a knowledge of the post-Cold War order. During the Cold War, states were often prepared to subordinate their own interests to the wider ideological interests of the bloc (Danilenko 1991). In the case of human rights, the benefits of keeping faith with the bloc far outweighed the costs. This solidarity enabled a well-defined consensus to emerge within each bloc, simplifying the politics of human rights by reducing the debate to little more than a straight-forward ideological struggle over prioritizing particular sets of rights that reflected the values of either socialism or capitalism. Disagreements within the bloc were therefore subsumed by a system that tended to mollify dissent on many issues, including human rights.

In the post-Cold War era, however, the shift from a bipolar to a multipolar international system, which is not as susceptible to bloc pressure, forces us to re-assess past assumptions on consensus, including that claimed for human rights. As states begin to exercise their sovereign independence, free of Cold War constraints, the necessity to support a particular view of human rights is less pressing. If this is correct, and the end of the Cold War signals a new assertiveness by sovereign independent states, then the positive consequences of the post-1989 order may not materialize and, for human rights in particular, may see old problems brought into even sharper focus (Donnelly 1994). Alston, for example, argues that the causes of the United Nations' failure to fulfil the promise of human rights are the same today as they were during the Cold War: the failure to afford economic and social rights parity with civil and political rights; the failure to acknowledge the limitations of international law; the failure to develop new techniques for preventing violations; the failure to come to terms with a dynamic international system, and the failure to confront the tensions between universal and particular claims (Alston 1994). Given the time and energy devoted to human rights at the United Nations during the last five decades, it seems reasonable to exclude apathy as the root cause of these failures. Instead, if the argument presented here is accepted – that power and interests define the dominant conception of human rights in any historic period – many of the problems of human rights are likely to remain unchanged, despite changes to world order.

While the context of the post-Cold War international era offers considerable scope for reflection on human rights, the new conditions of globalization add further complexity to our assessment of the future. Although it is common to find human rights commentators writing under the assumption that the post-Cold War order remains an order of states, over which the hegemony of the United States presides, a growing body of scholarly work argues that in the current period hegemony cannot be understood simply as the dominance of a single state. According to this thesis, in the age of globalization, power is located within what Cox has termed the *nébuleuse*, a group of formal and informal institutions without democratic pretensions (Cox 1995). Included in the *nébuleuse* are organizations like the World Bank, the International Monetary Fund, the World Trade Organization, the Trilateral Commission, Davos meetings and the Group of Seven. According to Cox and other globalization theorists, rather than understanding hegemony as a state-centric, core–periphery phenomenon (Wallerstein 1983), today hegemony describes a complex of non-territorial, core–periphery social relations that generate and sustain new patterns of economic growth and consumption (Cox 1994).

The conclusion drawn from this approach to globalization is that while the state continues to play a significant role in the new global order, the state no longer initiates policy but, rather, reacts to global forces against which it can mount little resistance (Held & McGrew 1999). The new role of the state under conditions of globalization is to act as a unit of administration, to orchestrate the conditions of globalization rather than to act as the independent political decision maker described by traditional theory. Furthermore, the development of a global free market in financial services, which represents another powerful characteristic of globalization, has restricted governments' scope to run deficits, causing major cuts in spending on health, education, housing, food subsidies and social welfare payments (UNDP 1997). As expressed by Panitch, in the age of globalization states are the 'authors of a regime that defines and guarantees, through international treaties and constitutional effect, the global and domestic rights of capital' (Panitch 1995: 85). Decisions made at the international level may temporarily disrupt patterns of globalization, but states cannot resist in the long term. Globalization has therefore diminished the state's traditional decision-making role, forced the privatization of key industries and services, and brought job cuts and increased levels of unemployment. Thus, the impact of globalization on human rights, particularly, but not exclusively, on economic and social rights, will have consequences for human rights that are not yet fully understood.

Given this analysis of the current global order, all issues of global politics must be subordinated to the imperatives of globalization, including human rights. Central to these imperatives are the principles of free market capitalism, which enjoins all countries to pursue economic growth and development above all other objectives (Robinson 1996; Rupert 1997). Under conditions of globalization, the traditionally conceived tensions between state sovereignty and individual rights are replaced by those between the imperatives of globalization and individual rights. Critics see evidence for this in the intolerance shown to those who attempt to reject the 'logic' of free market economics. Critics also point to the prejudice in favour of a conception of rights that continues to diminish the role of social and economic rights at the expense of civil and political freedoms. The examples of large-scale engineering projects that displace tens of thousands of people against their wishes, the ease with which governments overlook the violations of human rights perpetrated by important trading partners and the continued supply of military equipment to strategic allies regardless of their human rights record readily come to mind in this respect (Barber & Grainne 1993; Robinson 1993; Lawyers Committee 1992a).

Central to the globalization thesis is the issue of how to recon-ceptualize democracy in an era that has transformed the political economy role of the state, from one understood as primary decision maker to that of reactive facilitator (Gill 1996; Panitch 1995). Given that the non-democratic decisions of multinational corporations and international institutions touch the lives of people across the globe, it seems strange that questions of democratic participation and self-determinations remain largely unanswered. These questions are discussed in greater detail in Chapter 4. However, several points should be emphasized here, all of which cast doubt on the often assumed positive relationship between democracy and human rights.

The first is to reiterate the argument that under conditions of globalization the capabilities of the democratic state to pursue the wishes of its citizens are severely constrained (Held 1992, 1995). The second is to note that the recent enthusiasm of some states to abandon old authoritarian ways and embrace the idea of democracy does not necessarily mean that the human rights of citizens are any better protected (Gills, Rocamora & Wilson 1993). Third, we should question the liberal assertion that conducting economic and trade relationships necessarily has a 'civilizing' influence on those who violate human rights, an argument that both the British prime minister, Margaret Thatcher and President Ronald Reagan used to defend their policy towards apartheid South Africa (Evans 1999). Finally, we should question the role of aid and structural adjustment programmes in the context of development, human rights and democracy (Tomasevski 1993; Thomas 1998).

Globalization therefore challenges us to rethink many of the principles and concepts of the past and forces us to ask hard questions about their value within the current and future world order. Does globalization offer us an opportunity to develop a clear consensus on human rights? Are we really moving from the age of standard setting to the age of implementing human rights? Can we continue in the belief that the state remains the principal institution for protecting human rights in the age of globalization? Does international law offer the best hope for protecting human rights, or do we need to develop new systems of law best described as 'transnational law' (Evans & Hancock 1998)? Following from this, can the existing international organizations devoted to the protection of human rights be expected to fulfil the tasks they were created to perform or do they merely offer the appearance of progress? Although commentators often fête the spread of democracy, if our conception of participation remains limited to the national level, how do we expect this to support the demand for universal human rights? Globalization raises these and many other questions, some of which are examined in greater detail in the following chapters.

A further challenge to any programme for securing human rights is presented by the assumption that the forces of globalization are 'irresistible and irreversible' (Tony Blair, WTO, 19 May 1998). Taking this assumption at face value, many authoritarian governments have sought to defend their human rights record by arguing that they are powerless to resist the imperatives of economic growth and development, which often create the context for violations of human rights. These governments therefore plead for patience and leniency in judging their human rights records, arguing that their status as transition economies often produces circumstances that are not commensurate with their international obligations.

The plea for tolerance takes one of two forms: the 'stability' argument or the 'progress' argument. The 'stability' argument asserts that the legacy of colonialism has left many less developed states with the task of forging a nation from a diversity of religious, ethnic, racial and cultural groups, which brings the constant threat of conflicting interests, social unrest and political turmoil. To achieve stability, which is understood as a prerequisite for economic growth and development, governments may have to adopt repressive policies for dealing with factionalism, including the denial of certain human rights. The 'progress' argument asserts that in the name of social reform and democracy the less developed economies must achieve a rapid transformation from traditional to modern modes of production and consumption. It is therefore imperative that conservatives and traditionalists who resist the processes of modernization are swept aside in the interests of the nation and future generations (Tamilmoran 1992). If this means that governments cannot always fulfil their human rights obligations, then the world should exercise patience and understanding as nations respond to the imperatives of globalization with actions that foster the birth of mature economic and political systems.

Either or both arguments might be invoked, for example, if a community is forcibly moved from its traditional lands to accommodate a large-scale infrastructual development or in cases where brutal police and military intervention is used to put down peaceful resistance to industrial developments that threaten to pollute tribal farmland (Christian Aid 1996; UNPO 2000). Accordingly, nation building, modernization, economic progress and the common good are used as a defence against accusations of human rights violations. If development strategies, investment programmes and trade agreements do lead to violations of human rights, then international society should be tolerant in the name of stability and progress (Johnston & Button 1994).

Some of these issues concerned with the post-Cold War era and globalization are identifiable in the recent appeal to 'Asian values'. Asian countries first articulated their alternative approach to human rights at a regional conference in Bangkok during 1993, preparatory to the United Nations-sponsored conference on human rights held in Vienna. The declaration that emerged from the Bangkok meeting affirmed the sovereign authority of the state as a bulwark against the West's proclivity for imperialist control by meddling in the internal affairs of Asian states. Furthermore, while the declaration accepts the universality of human rights, it seeks to promote a conception founded on a set of explicitly Asian values, which stresses the importance of national and regional particularities and the historical, cultural, social and religious contexts of Asia (Arrigo 1993; Alston 1994). This will be discussed in further detail in Chapter 4.

While the post-Cold War order and the conditions of globalization play a considerable part in setting the new context for human rights, the tradition of individualism continues to obscure our vision of the structural causes of violations (Galtung 1994). Within the human rights debate, scholars and practitioners routinely take the individual as both the claimant of rights and the perpetrator of violations. The priority afforded to civil and political rights supports the interests of free market principles, which seek to promote a socio-economic environment in which innovation, endeavour and enterprise are highly prized. Given this understanding and purpose of personal freedom, it follows that we must also hold the individual responsible for all of his or her actions, including violations of human rights. This convention, which has its roots in the Judeo-Christian notion of sin, tends to deflect attention from those economic, social and political structures that support the interests of particular groups. Consequently, investigations into the causes of human rights violations seldom go beyond the assumption that all violations can be explained by reference to the wilful acts of evil, brutal, despotic and cruel individuals, excluding the possibility, for example, that the principles of international politics, the rules that govern world trade or the principles of the global economic order itself may also lead to human rights violations.

Noting that the practices associated with the current structures of the global economy cause many violations of human rights does not suggest that individuals are not, on occasion, responsible for heinous crimes against humanity or that evil does not exist.

However, it does raise questions about current approaches to implementing rights. For example, if the current structures and practices of globalization do cause many violations, the emphasis given to a system of implementation that seeks to identify human rights violators, bring them to trial and administer punishments seems misplaced. As Johan Galtung has pointed out, structures cannot be juridical persons with intentions and capabilities, nor can they be arrested, put before a court and punished for their crimes (Galtung 1994). The international law applies only to identifiable actions, not social institutions and legitimate practices that provide the context for action. Similarly, Tomasevski has observed that international law may have the capability to redress consequences but it cannot address causes (Tomasevski 1993; see also Chinkin 1998). The creation of a permanent International Criminal Court, following the experience of tribunals for the former Yugoslavia and Rwanda, may therefore have little impact on protecting human rights (Fatic 2000).

It might, of course, be argued that notwithstanding the weakness of international courts and tribunals in addressing structural causes of violations, they none the less provide a powerful deterrent. While this argument may have some limited force, experience demonstrates that politics often intervenes, exposing courts and tribunals to charges of inconsistency. Why, for example, was a tribunal set up to prosecute those responsible for crimes against humanity in the former Yugoslavia but not for those who ordered the bombing of defeated and retreating troops on the road to Basra during the Gulf War? We might also ask why the powers given to the tribunal on the former Yugoslavia, which permits the 'arrest if encountered' of indicted individuals, are widely interpreted as 'avoid encounter at all costs' (Robinson 1997). General Mladic and Radovan Kardzic still 'roam freely in the Republika Srbska despite the fact that it is patrolled by NATO troops' (Daly 1997). What little deterrent effect courts and tribunals may have is severely weakened by such actions.

Finally, the conclusion to draw from the above discussion is that an enduring consensus on human rights remains elusive. Many commentators would refute the analysis offered above on the grounds that in the post-Cold War era human rights and human dignity have at last achieved a genuinely universal acceptance, based upon a concept of the 'common good'. According to these arguments, the triumph of capitalism over Marxism and socialism paves the way for all peoples to enjoy the fruits of democracy, which will guarantee global justice, human rights and human security. The ideologically motivated conflicts of difference that characterized the Cold War are over. Instead, the new order is marked by a global consensus on the purposes and principles of economic, social and political life, which are understood in terms of a single global history. However, as Pasha and Blaney have argued, these conclusions are, at the very least, premature:

> We need not appeal to a conception of unassimilable differences to make this point. We need only gesture to the contested status of human rights within world politics, to debates about the nature of democracy, or to disputes about who can speak for nature and the implications for the character of the human relationship to the environment, in order to suggest that consensus is mostly lacking. Or we might point to the contested status of the very idea of a cosmopolitan view of justice? Or we might simply ask: how does one know, short of the global democracy that TAL [transnational associational life] is said to be in the process of creating, that a consensus exists? (Pasha & Blaney 1998: 436)

In this view, ideas of consensus and the common good may be little more than the assertions of those who benefit most from a particular conception of human rights, democracy and environmental security. In short, notions of a consensus and the common good are never free of power and should be scrutinized within the context of power.

Symbolic of the triumph of interests, as opposed to that of the common good, is the United States' ratification of the ICCPR, following decades of a policy not to ratify any international law on human rights. While at first sight the United States' ratification appears to signal the end of its historic objections to accepting any human rights treaty that did not reflect exactly the rights set out in the Constitution, and a willingness to lend hegemonic support for the formal global human rights regime, on closer inspection this may not be the case. Importantly, critics argue that the ratification is little more than an attempt to attract the moral status attached to the treaty without accepting any of its obligations. According to critics, this was achieved by the cynical use of reservations, declarations and derogations, a system that allows a state party to a treaty to reject, restrict and redefine particular obligations articulated in that treaty. Notable among these in the United States' ratification is the federal government's declaration that the Covenant does not come into effect until Congress has passed the necessary legislation, a device that avoids historic arguments about the treaty-making powers of the president and the imposition of new social norms on the states (Evans 1996).

The influential Lawyers Committee on Human Rights has observed, for example, that the limitations set by the reservations, declarations and derogations in the United States' ratification, reinforces the US's historic policy on human rights. Thus, the Lawyers Committee argues that the US's ratification is 'hypocritical' because it suggests 'one set of rules applies to the United States and another to the rest of the world' (Lawyers Committee 1992b). In a similar vein, the prominent US international lawyer Louis Henkin has accused the United States of seeking moral legitimacy without accepting any international obligations, arguing that the ratification re-affirms the historic record, that is, human rights conventions are for 'other states, not the United States' (Henkin 1995: 433). The UN Human Rights Committee also articulated its own concerns following the ratification, although without explicitly naming the United States. In a 1994 report, the Committee expressed its dissatisfaction with reservations that 'essentially render ineffective all Covenant rights which would require any changes to national law to ensure compliance' so that 'no real international rights or obligations have been accepted' (Human Rights Committee 1994). The United States is currently considering ratifying the ICESCR, which would certainly suffer from the same, if not greater, limitations.

Conclusion

The aim of this chapter was to explore the politics of rights, particularly the important role of power in human rights talk. It was argued that although rights are often expressed in the language of moral philosophy, the current status of the global human rights regime has more to do with legitimacy, conflict and struggle. This argument was developed within the context of the politics of the UDHR, the ICCPR and the ICESCR. It was further developed within the context of the post-Cold War era, which was understood as the age of globalization. Accepting that the politics of rights plays an important role in determining the types of rights we can claim, and the institution through which claims might be made, allows us to understand rights as both sustaining existing forms of dominance and providing a powerful tool with which to challenge those forms (Stammers 1995). It also helps explain why proponents of rights often seem over-optimistic while critics often seem over-pessimistic. Finally, it was argued that, given the dynamism of politics and society, rights should be understood as a process that reflects particular historic configurations of power relations. We should therefore attempt to understand human rights within the context of the new post-Cold War order and the dynamic context of globalization, which creates new problems for the struggle for rights.

The next chapter will look in more detail at the place of human rights in the world-view that has dominated the thinking of international relations scholars and statespeople in recent years. It also explores further some of the themes sketched out above, including globalization and the role of international law.

CHAPTER 2

International Human Rights Law and Global Politics

This chapter looks at the politics of international human rights law. It begins by examining the place of international law in the tradition of Realist international theory, which attempts to view any rule-governed behaviour as the outcome of hegemony. In this approach to international politics, international law is little more than an attempt to legitimate the interests of powerful states. Inasmuch as human rights plays any role in this process, it does so because it serves the hegemon's interests, not because of concern for human security and dignity. A further section looks at the role of international law in international society approaches to interstate politics. In contrast to Realism, these approaches give greater prominence to international law as the expression of a normative order that rejects understanding international politics as a sphere dominated by the self-regarding, egoistic and self-interested state. Instead, international society is a realm in which states agree to conform to certain patterns of behaviour that allow predictability, stability and the prospect of peaceful coexistence. Legitimacy is achieved when states abide by these rules, which may include fulfilling those obligations undertaken in international human rights law.

A third section looks at the role of international law under conditions of globalization. It argues that the changing role of sovereignty within the present global order raises important questions about the potency of international institutions developed in a previous period, including the institutions of international law. It argues that if globalization theory is correct, and the state no longer enjoys its status as the single most important actor on the global stage, the emphasis on law that governs relations between states is misplaced. For human rights, which are based upon the principles of universality, this has serious consequences. The final section discusses the near singularity of international law as the best means for securing human rights. It suggests that the stress on international human rights law as the best means for protecting human rights is misplaced within the economic, social and political contexts of globalization. This is for two reasons: first, in the age of globalization the state has less capacity to deliver human rights; and second, the application of legal norms and processes cannot alter the global structural contexts in which many violations take place. Although the focus on international law offers an illusion of orderliness and progress in the field of human rights, and in doing so deflects attention from structural causes of violations, globalization means that international law cannot deliver on its promises.

The Role of International Law in International Relations

International Law and International Political Realism

International political Realism has dominated the thinking of academics, diplomats and statespeople for much of the period since the end of the Second World War. Although other approaches have achieved some prominence during recent years, Realism still provides the guiding principles for much of the theory and practice of international relations. Realism begins by making a distinction between political and international theory. According to this distinction, political theory is concerned with some notion of the 'good life' (Wight 1966), generated by a culturally specific, ideal moral community with shared values and beliefs. Cultural and historical specificity supports the claim to sovereignty, which includes the associated principles of self-determination, non-intervention, domestic jurisdiction and autonomy. The assumption of these principles focuses attention on normative relationships between the institutions of government and the governed in the search to create the conditions for the 'good life' within the sovereign territorial state. Political theory is therefore concerned with normative relationships between the institutions of governance and the governed.

If the task of political theory is to describe existing social and political relationships within the state, to investigate alternatives and to present proposals for perfecting existing forms of the state (Jackson 1990), international theory is concerned with ways of securing the internal order from external interference. According to Realist thinking, the claims to sovereignty, self-determination, domestic jurisdiction and non-intervention lead to an international order best described as anarchical. It is anarchical because states are engaged in a relentless struggle to protect their own sovereign peoples through the aggregation of power and resources. In this way the state seeks to guarantee the freedom of its citizens, to pursue the national interest and to promote the interests of its people. As John Hertz argued many years ago, international theory is concerned with discovering the best means for protecting the 'hard shell' of the state and securing its distinctive social, political and economic order within an anarchical international system (Hertz 1954). Put simply by Walker, the distinction between political and international theory is best described as:

> Community inside, anarchy outside; justice inside, power and, at best, order outside; effective institutions with legislative authority inside, shifting alliances and fragile balancing mechanisms outside – however normal politics is understood, interstate politics may be presented as its negation. (Walker 1990)

This view of the international order is trenchant inasmuch as it reflects a widely held understanding of international politics, which finds expression in both popular imagery and the utterances of statespeople and diplomats, although not necessarily expressed consciously.

For many Realist thinkers, the field of international relations is best described as a system because it displays regular interactions between sovereign states operating under conditions of international anarchy, interactions understood as conforming to timeless, habitual and unchanging rules. These rules are said to derive from an axiomatic notion that the pursuit of coercive power is the best means of securing the normative order within the state. International relations are therefore driven by conflict, self-interest and the need to prevail. However, because power is distributed unevenly within the international system, hegemonic states assume responsibility for performing the necessary tasks associated with maintaining world order. This privileged position allows the hegemon to promote its moral preferences as value-free, neutral, impartial and objective: as 'common-sense' values that serve the interests of all states and peoples, not merely those of the hegemon (Gramsci 1996). As argued in Chapter 1, according to Realists, 'hegemonic logic' determines that even issues that pay no respect to territorial boundaries, like human rights and environmental degradation, must be subordinated to the interests of the hegemon.

The enduring and unchanging quality of the Realists' world of international relations, which emphasizes power, self-interest and anarchy, raises important questions about existing forms of cooperation and rule-governed behaviours that, at first sight, appear to deny the self-seeking activities of states. Since Realists argue that all forms of action must be understood within the context of power relations, the creation of international law, including that on human rights, must be recognized for its political quality. As Stein has argued, the Realist understanding of international relations 'suggests that the same forces of autonomously calculated self-interest that lie at the root of the anarchic international system also lay the foundations for regimes as forms of international law' (Stein 1982: 316). Since the Realists' tradition rejects any potential for the anarchical international order of states to undergo a transformation into a world society – a society of people sharing a common history – the creation and efficacy of international law on human rights depends upon the interests of the hegemon.

This approach to international law is reflected in *The Twenty Years' Crisis*, arguably the central text of international Realism. In this E.H. Carr asserts that international law, 'like politics, is a meeting place for ethics and power ... it cannot be understood independently of the political foundations in which it rests and of the political interests which it serves' (Carr 1939: 178–9). The principal purpose of international law is to maintain the conditions for order, including economic cooperation, conflict resolution and respect for sovereignty. Accordingly, international law should strive to 'preserve the interstate world of judicially equal members' and thus the interests of those who most benefit from sustaining the international system of states (Mosler 1980: 5–4). Under the rubric of Realism, 'international legitimacy and sovereignty are a function of whether a government politically controls the population, rather then whether it justly represents the people' (Teśon 1992: 53). Thus, the right to a voice in creating international law is not predicated upon a legitimacy derived from social representation but from the claim to sustain the principles of the international system. Oppenheim's observation, that the 'so-called rights of man not only do not, but cannot enjoy any protection under international law, because the law is concerned solely with the relationship between states and cannot confer rights on individuals' (quoted in Robinson & Merrills 1992: 3), remains a central tenet of Realism.

International Law and International Society

Although for many scholars the explanatory power of Realism remains trenchant, in more recent times it has come under considerable attack for not reflecting the reality of the current world order. Noting that the state alone cannot perform all the tasks associated with providing the conditions for the 'good life', and that the expansion of the global economy demands greater interdependence, some scholars have sought to moderate the tension between anarchy and society found at the centre of Realism. The spread of technology, the development of regional and global international organizations, the increasing mobility of capital and finance and the growing complexity of economic, social and political life are said to promote the conditions favourable for an international society, a society more concerned with cooperation and less with conflict, hegemony and the imperative to prevail (Keohane 1984). However, greater global interdependence also brings its own problems, most notably global environmental degradation, international terrorism, international crime and, as we shall see in the following chapters, new threats to human rights. Consequently, there is a growing awareness that both the material and social well-being of people everywhere depends upon social, political and economic relationships that transcend traditional state boundaries. According to proponents of interdependence, given this new context of international relations, Realism cannot account for recent developments in world order. Instead, some scholars argue that international relations are now better characterized as an international society, a community of sovereign states sharing certain common values, aspirations and a vision of the 'good life'.

The emergence of the concept of international society sharing common values suggests that a normative order exists both within sovereign states and, at the international level, between states. However, proponents of international society draw a qualitative distinction between the two. Terry Nardin, for example, has suggested that while international law does provide a considerable measure of normative order that belies the moral scepticism of Realism, a distinction should be drawn between the 'purposive association' common to national societies and the 'practical association' that describes international society (Nardin 1983). Following the distinction between political and international theory discussed earlier, Nardin argues that the existence of a domestic normative order presupposes a moral community possessed of a set of common values, norms and rules. The domestic normative order therefore rests upon some notion of a common purpose, which assumes the moral integrity of the individual within a culturally specific social environment that includes a commonly held view of the 'good life'. However, because of cultural diversity and the existence of sovereign states, Nardin argues that

> ... it would be a mistake to regard all international relations as defined and governed by the pursuit of shared purpose ... there is another mode of relations that is more fundamental because it exists among those pursuing divergent as well as shared purpose. Durable relations among adversaries presupposes a framework of common practices and rules capable of providing some unifying bond where shared purpose is lacking. (Nardin 1983: 5)

These are the non-purposive rules of 'practical association', the most important expression of which are found in the authoritative practices and principles of international law. Such rules require no commitment to shared purposes or values, but they do provide a formal unity, an association of states, based upon restraint and accommodation. Practical association occurs when those who fail to get others to adopt their own values 'have little choice but to tolerate the existence of differences they are unable to eradicate' (Nardin 1983: 57). In short, the purpose of international law is to 'preserve the interstate world of judicially equal members', to maintain peace and promote cooperation between states, not to challenge the values that define domestic society (Mosler 1980: 5–6).

Nardin's formulation reinforces the tendency to objectify the state in similar fashion to Realism. If the rules of practical association are devoid of any moral purpose, international society is morally problematic. The rules of practical association are the concern of the state and the institutions of international society, where the principles associated with sovereignty act as an effective barrier to any form of intervention for promoting or protecting universal values, human rights included. Moreover, Nardin's analysis seems to suggest that international law serves all states equally, overlooking arguments about the role of power and interests in law making and implementation at both the domestic and international level (Collins 1990; Chimni 1999; Hoffman 1988). While the members of international society are considered equal as subjects under international law, politics, power and interests continue to settle the agenda in which international law plays its role.

Furthermore, the modern state is not a fact of nature, but an historic response to the emergence of a new social order, first recognized during the seventeenth century and later stimulated by the Industrial Revolution (Linklater 1990). Against this, the international society approach attempts to view all problems through a prism of familiarity, as though we live in an unchanging (indeed, unchangeable) world. Nardin and other international society scholars can therefore be criticized for offering a conservative approach to international law. It is conservative because it fails to acknowledge the dynamic nature of global social, political and economic interactions that generate new forms of social exchange, including new forms of state (Cox 1981), which have little to do with past conceptions of sovereignty (Bateson 1990). For many commentators, evidence for this dynamism is seen in the growing authority of non-state actors, who assume responsibility for implementing international law and coordinating the processes associated with generating new rules. This trend, which Herman Mosler has called 'relative sovereignty', is said to circumscribe state power and reduces the state's capability to perform all the tasks that the international society approach currently associates with sovereignty (Mosler 1980). While such a view may offer some encouragement to those who see sovereignty as the greatest barrier to achieving the universal implementation of human rights, it remains unclear how the tradition of separating domestic from international politics will give way to 'relative sovereignty' on human rights issues.

Nardin's distinction between purposive and practical association also lends further support to the notion that international law is value-free, at least in as far as the application of the rules requires no commitment to a moral purpose beyond a need to maintain order. At the international level, justice is concerned with equality before the law or the equal application of the rules, not with securing a just outcome, which might require discrimination in favour of the least advantaged. Furthermore, the 'law of nations' remains the law governing relations between states, not the law common to all nations, which suggests a global moral community of humankind. Consequently, the option to disregard the rules, in preference for the pursuit of self-interest, does not attract moral disapprobation of the same quality that we would expect to find at the domestic level, where purposive rules operate. Accordingly, Fernando Teśon has argued:

> The enlightened moral and political global reality is ill-served by the statist model of international law. The model promotes states and not individuals, governments not persons, order not rights, compliance not justice. It insists that rulers be permitted to exercise whatever amount of coercion is necessary to politically control their subjects. (Teśon 1992: 101)

One further assumption made by proponents of international society should also be mentioned. This argument asserts that human rights issues are now so high on the international political agenda that no state can afford to ignore questions of rights in its foreign policy. In observing this, proponents of international society seek not merely to note an important supplement to the foreign policy agenda but to claim that the legitimate member of international society must demonstrate a commitment to human rights. Today, it is argued, it is not enough for a state to claim sovereignty in accordance with the principles of self-determination alone. Instead, the legitimate state is expected actively to uphold the human rights of its citizens and promote human rights in its foreign dealings (Vincent 1986). Accordingly, human rights are protected within international society because they are 'constitutive of the international definition of a legitimate nation-state', they are not merely 'privileges graciously granted by individuals in power – for example, by signing an international human rights convention' (Teśon 1992: 83). This is not to argue that the consensus on human rights is such that human rights claims now take priority over sovereignty. However, it does provide a strong argument for those who think that strengthening the institutions of international society can resolve the tension between the principles of sovereignty and the doctrine of universal human rights.

The response to this argument is to look at the distinction between the obligations set out in the global human rights regime, which most states acknowledge formally, and the actual behaviour of states, which often indicates a failure to live up to those obligations. Noting this disjuncture is problematic for proponents of international society because society not only infers some set of common values but also some means for sanctioning those who offend against those values, in this case rules that are said to bring sovereign legitimacy. However, no such sanctions exist at the level of international society:

> If states or other participants in international politics fail to meet the standards set, what are or should be the consequences? Invasion? Armed support for justifiable revolution? Economic intervention? Persuasion? Indifference? Or a pointed stare in the opposite direction (when it comes to enforcement) in order not to ruffle sovereign feathers? (Vincent 1986: 132)

Since no consensus exists on the legitimate means to enforce even the most important rules that are said to define the membership of international society, the assertion that international society offers a better chance for protecting human rights is unclear.

In recent years a branch of theory closely related to international society theory has received wide interest (Evans & Wilson 1992). Manifestations of international cooperation are characterized as international regimes, understood as sets of principles, norms, rules and decision-making procedures accepted by states as a guide for international action in a given issue-area of international relations (Krasner 1983). Although theorists argue that international regimes are best understood as institutions, and are therefore concerned with the customs and habits found in social life, they are often closely associated with international organizations charged with the task of overseeing the conduct of states in relation to their obligations under international law. For example, it is common to see references to the trade regime when discussing the World Trade Organization. Similarly, discussion of the global human rights regime usually centres on the activities of the Commission for Human Rights, the United Nations Economic and Social Council and other United Nations agencies with an interest in human rights, notably the International Labour Organisation. In common with the international society approach, regime theory asserts that the reasons behind the move to create international institutions with responsibility for so many aspects of economic, social and political life is growing complexity, the growth of information technology and rapid economic expansion. However, even as members of regimes, states continue to assume the role of principal actors in world politics, resisting the claims of *supra*-state groups to wrest sovereignty from them. In the words of the main architect of international society thinking, states remain the principal bearers of rights and duties under international law, 'they alone have the right to use force to uphold it' and 'its source lies in the consent of states expressed in custom and treaty' (Bull 1977: 68).

The international society approach to international relations does not therefore seem to offer any better prospects for delivering human rights. The sovereign state remains the central actor; international law, characterized as a neutral body of rules, is the principal instrument of global governance, and the potential for change in the structures of world order is severely limited. While the idea of human rights may have achieved an elevated position in political imagery, the methods for implementing them remain limited by the social, economic and political institutions of a past era.

The question then remains, is the global order so unchanging that the prospects for human rights are limited? Recently, interest in globalization has suggested that the constraints of sovereignty on developing new social, economic and political relations are either in decline or at least undergoing processes of transformation. If this is so, then any attempt to protect human rights through international law seems even less likely to succeed. The objectification of the state and the stress given to international law allows a separation of human rights violations from the generality of global social behaviour, practice and knowledge described by globalization (Dalby 1992). Furthermore, the objectification of the state leads to viewing all issues, including human rights, as technical-legal problems, decoupling them from the current global social and political order. Instead of asking why violations of human rights continue to occur on a global scale, which would include an assessment of structural causes of violations, attention is focused on the sites of violations and identifying those responsible for atrocities. Social, economic and political practices are rarely factored into the analysis of human rights violations, which leaves those who benefit from these practices free of all moral responsibility. In short, the reification of the state leads to an undynamic view of world politics, creating a disjuncture between the optimism generated by international law and the reality of global politics, a disjuncture that represents an obstacle to change (Dalby 1992).

Globalization, International Law and Human Rights

Although the centre–periphery, world system analysis developed by Wallerstein many years ago might be seen in retrospect as an early attempt to understand the global, political economy dimensions of world order, today globalization is seen as something more than structural relationships based upon a state-centric view of world politics (Wallerstein 1983). Instead, globalization infers social relationships where the social core and the social periphery cut across national boundaries, creating new patterns of economic growth and consumption that are beyond the control of the state (Gill 1995). While in the previous phase of world history the state could adopt national strategies for ordering the national economy, including the nationalization of key industries, the global organization of production and finance means that states 'by and large play the role of agencies of the global economy, with the task of adjusting national economic policies and practices to the perceived exigencies of global economic liberalism' (Cox 1999: 12).

This is not to suggest that the state is in terminal decline, a conclusion that most globalization theorists reject, and which was first encountered in Chapter 1. Instead, globalization theory argues that the state is assuming a new and integral role as an administrative unit for creating and orchestrating the conditions for further globalization. Rather than remaining the central actors on the global stage, today states create and manage a global order that supports the rights of domestic and global capital (Panitch 1995). In this way the 'future prosperity of transnational corporations and financial institutions depends not only upon the context of competition in the global market but also on an ability to influence the rules that govern the market' (Wilson 1997). The creation and implementation of international law plays a central role in this process. Decisions made at the national level may disrupt patterns of globalization on occasion, but states cannot escape its consequences for long.

Globalization acknowledges that although the development of a global economy is not a new phenomenon (Hirst & Thompson 1996), the introduction of new technology, in particular information technology, accelerates processes of change associated with social integration and disintegration and inclusion and exclusion. On the one hand, globalization enables the organiza-tion of production and finance on a global scale, encouraging the formation of a transnational class whose identities, loyalties and social bonds owe more to the global political economy than to state citizenship (van der Pijl 1998). On the other hand, globalization theory suggests that these rapid changes in patterns of production and consumption challenge the traditional social relations, beliefs and values upon which ideas of community are built. Consequently, globalization interrogates the old categories of international political thought, raises questions about identity and community and further confuses the distinction between domestic and international politics (Gill 1995).

An ideology of modernity underpins the shift to a global economy, which rests upon the twin goals of economic growth and development, defined as global capital accumulation and consumption. The central means of achieving these goals in all countries, whether the wealthy North or the impoverished South, is strategic planning at the global level, global management and the creation of global regimes and agreements. Ideological convergence has the effect of homogenizing and limiting the policy choices of governments. Global management requires adherence to rules that ensure all countries conform to the development model so that the 'hidden hand' of the market can operate efficiently. Consequently, responsibility for defining and implementing the rules of international action shifts away from the state to international institutions and regimes.

Although the demand for human rights is, in part, the outcome of an ideology of modernity, all issues must be subordinated to the imperatives of economic growth and development. Indeed, this subordination is expressed through the rights debate itself. Specifically, the defence of property rights over and above social and welfare rights privileges the accumulation of capital at the expense of distributive policies that would have empowered the poor. The 1960 UN resolution calling for a 'speedy and unconditional end to colonialism in all its forms and manifestations' offers an early example of this. Although few countries failed to support the resolution, the United States abstained, arguing that the resolution would damage corporate interests, particularly the claim to the proprietorship over subsoil deposits (Haas 1970). More recently, the US's approach to environmental issues served the same purpose (Chatterjee & Finger 1994).

Further examples are not difficult to find. Barber and Grainne report that 'thirty to forty per cent of the ten million people who have been resettled to make way for large dams in China since the 1950s are still impoverished and lack adequate food and clothing' (Barber & Grainne 1993: 24). More recently, the Indian government plans to forcibly move tens of thousands of people who live in the flood region created by the Narmada Dam project.

The massacre of at least fifty East Timorese by Indonesian troops in 1991 led to threats from aid donors to discontinue economic aid. However, the importance of trade soon took precedence over human rights (Robinson 1993). Further and more detailed examples of the priority given to economics over human rights will be given in the next chapter.

The changing role of the state under conditions of globalization, together with the dominance of the liberal free market system, also brings consequences for the relationship between human rights and political participation. As the state increasingly assumes the character of a passive unit of administration, rather than that of an active policy maker, the result is a decline in the capacity of people to participate in defining a political agenda that expresses a genuine concern for human rights. For example, when a finance minister argues that the devaluation of a currency was the result of global market forces beyond government control, rather than the failure of national economic planning, as the British Chancellor of the Exchequer, Norman Lamont did in 1992, the disjuncture between political participation and power is exposed. People begin to question what political participation means if their elected government is impotent in exercising any control over important economic factors that affect their prosperity and daily lives.

With the realization that the global economy, rather than the national economy, exercises greater influence on economic well-being, the state loses its significance as a centre of authority through which people can express their preferences. Instead, the focus turns to international institutions and organizations, who assume the task of providing the rules for action. Although governments continue to engage in international politics, governance is conducted by a group of formal and informal organizations, the *nébuleuse* (Cox 1995), whose task is to provide and maintain the conditions for capital expansion. The move to gain legitimacy for rules that free global capital from all spacial and temporal constraints is significant because 'all the noted texts [e.g. those related to the WTO] confer or hope to bestow a number of rights on transnational capital [but] ... impose no corresponding duties' (Chimni 1999: 339). The World Trade Organization is sometimes seen as the most advanced model for securing the interests of capital because it is the first global organization with the authority to 'strike down particular national interests, even when these are enshrined in law or custom' (George 1999: 22). Symbolic of this shift of power is the equal status given to 'corporate logos of every stripe [which] are on display alongside national flags' at Davos meetings as noted in a report by the US Public Broadcasting System (PBS) in 1998. The link between government and the governed is therefore weakened but not replaced with new forms of participation related to the global institutions of governance (Huymans 1995).

Over time, the decline in participation, coupled with the maintenance of an order in which the governed have no role, ensures that people become more accountable to remote centres of authority, rather than those centres being accountable to people. This is the process of 'distanciation', where 'locals are thoroughly penetrated by and shaped in terms of social influences quite distant from them' (Giddens 1990). Distanciation ensures the relationship between international institutions and populations is not concerned with human rights, human values, the quality of life or human dignity, but with technical issues to do with maintaining an order that supports free market principles, economic growth, development and profit. The programme to create intellectual property rights offers a good example here. Such rights are more concerned with the rights of ownership, capital and the commodification of the environment than with social issues concerning the moral consequences of biotechnology and the potential for privatizing life forms (Gill 1995).

Structural Adjustment Programmes (SAPs) typify the redistribution of structural decision-making powers away from states and into global economic institutions, such as the World Bank and the International Monetary Fund (IMF). SAPs were initiated in the 1980s by the World Bank, ostensibly to support those countries suffering balance-of-payments results, mainly in the developing world. SAPs come with conditionality agreements that typically demand major cuts in government expenditure, including cutting down or abolishing important social programmes in education, health, housing and public sector development. In this way the Bank takes responsibility for the economic coordination of the state, and largely ignores any implications for economic, social and democratic rights. SAPs therefore deny 'human rights to food, education, work and social assistance' and render such claims meaningless (Tomasevski 1993: 61). Thus, 'the interests of global financial and corporate institutions are privileged over that of popular, national or redistributive goals' (Gills 1995), offering powerful transnational corporations a further opportunity to gain influence over state policy at the expense of citizens' rights. As Galtung has observed, 'There may well be situations when the state can do without popular consent, but not without corporations in general and the banks in particular' (Galtung 1994: 149). In this way international law is 'playing an unprecedented role in creating and congealing inequalities in the international system':

> No longer confined to questions of war and peace or diplomacy, international law has, on the one hand, come to govern the use

of oceans and outer space, and on the other, regulate core aspects of national economic, social and cultural life. (Chimni 1999: 337)

If the analysis offered by globalization theory is trenchant, the prospects for gaining protection for human rights through international law seem bleak. The focus of international regulation is concerned with technical issues to do with maintaining the conditions of the global free market, not with human rights and dignity (Chimni 1999). Inasmuch as human rights do figure prominently on the agenda of global politics, the debate adopts a problem-solving perspective that seeks to deal with the unavoidable consequences of the current world order. Questions to do with the legitimacy of an order that itself provides the conditions for human rights violations are seldom raised. Indeed, the current world order is now so widely accepted as natural and inevitable that it has attained the status of 'common sense' (Augelli & Murphy 1988), suggesting that we must accept human rights violations as an unfortunate and inescapable consequence of human development. The role of international law is, at best, to provide a formal framework for human rights talk, not to challenge the current economic and political world order. While on occasion international law may claim some success in finding justice for those whose rights have been violated, it has little to contribute to challenging an order that constitutes a major source of human rights violations.

In conclusion, the role of international law is to legitimate the 'technical fix' that supports particular global interests. International law is part of the problem-solving process associated with the current world order – an order defined by the global economy in which the role of the state is to act as facilitator. For those with an interest in taking human rights seriously, globalization suggests that we should stand aside from the familiar and attempt to take a critical, more reflective view about the nature of hegemony, power, justice, public goods and processes of social change (Cox 1981). The failure to take this step leads to an over-reliance on international law solutions that cannot hope to achieve the aim of protecting human rights. The prevailing debates surrounding international human rights law are directed at achieving limited goals that do not disrupt the prevailing global order. Through conducting these debates in familiar terms that continue to understand the state as the dominant actor within the global political economy, lawyers, academics and human rights activists act as though the principles of world politics are unchangeable (Hoffman 1987). Rather than reflecting on the potential for change and the need to challenge the 'common-sense' notion of world order, the human rights debate contents itself with the limited success offered by international law.

The Limitations of International Human Rights Law

Following from the above discussion, within the current context of international theory, international law does not appear to offer the prospects to protect human rights that it promises. From the Realist and international society approaches to international relations, international law seems to offer only limited solutions to the continuing reports of human rights violations. When the conditions of globalization are factored into the analysis, including the limitations on the capacity of the state to intervene in important areas of the political economy where many causes of human rights violations are located, the potential of international law is severely limited. Indeed, those who accept the globalization thesis argue that we should reassess all the established institutions of global politics as we enter the next millennium, not just international law. The conclusion we should draw from globalization is that so long as international lawyers, academics and political leaders act as though we live in unchanging times, and fail to recognize that the cherished principles of the past may not provide a safe foundation for future decision making, the protection of human rights is likely to remain unfulfilled.

The reluctance to take this step is seen in the predisposition of lawyers, academics and statespeople for formalism, empiricism and written evidence. When assessing a particular case of human rights violations, these groups routinely turn to a detailed analysis of the covenants, protocols, conventions, declarations and procedures that constitute the international human rights regime. They seldom follow an alternative approach that attempts to analyse the social, political and economic context of violations. The reasons for this are found in the assumption that international law is value free, in contrast to the social and political sciences. First, it is argued that the interpretative methodologies often used by social and political scientists are open to the charge of value-bias, epistemological confusion and simple misunderstandings. To seek a foundation for decision making in these disciplines is therefore unsound. The second criticism focuses upon the problem of collecting reliable data, which is particularly arduous in the atmosphere of secrecy that often pervades the violation of human rights. Governments, international organizations and corporations are rarely enthusiastic to open themselves to investigations that might expose them to national and international vilification. Although non-governmental organizations (NGOs) have achieved some measure of success in overcoming this difficulty, and often publish reports that expose governments and corporations as human rights violators, NGOs are too easily dismissed as 'political' actors with little legitimacy. Faced with these methodological difficulties, those interested in the protection of human rights turn instead to the safety of legal material. However, the warning offered by Michael Barkun many years ago, that 'a narrow concern for the assertions of documents or for the power of legally constituted organs of government mistakes appearances for reality, confuses visibility for significance and substitutes (however inadvertently) sophisticated description for explanation', attracts little attention (Barkun 1968: 102).

International law has, however, achieved the status of 'common sense' for those who understand the theory and practice of human rights within the framework offered by international society. Such a 'common-sense' view tends to close the minds of decision makers to any critical appraisal of the emerging world order, which leaves many unanswered questions about the efficacy and value of current thinking on the protection of human rights. Rather than accepting that the continued failure to protect human rights reflects the failure to address the social, political and economic causes of violations, 'common sense' determines that we need even more international law to correct earlier shortcomings. In this way, human rights are treated as a legal-technical issue, which requires no analysis of political, economic and social contexts, legitimacy or interests (Young 1989; Stammers 1999). As expressed by one commentator, the international law approach to human rights means that 'only the form of the legal concept is considered while its content – the social reality it is supposed to express – is lost sight of' (Chimni 1999: 339). Similarly, Boyle has likened the 'common-sense' view of international law to the *choists*, a branch of French literature that devotes space to describing 'things' in an attempt to contrast the infinite quality of human aspirations with the unfeeling indifference of the world of brute objects (Boyle 1985). Thus, those who pin their hopes on international law overlook the reality that international law itself is a consequence of traditional, state-centric thinking on global politics and cannot be expected to resolve the more damaging consequences of an emerging, alternative global order.

Finally, it is worth recalling an argument first encountered in Chapter 1 to do with the centrality of the individual in the international law of human rights, both as a claimant and a potential violator, which the recent agreement to set up an International Criminal Court emphasizes. The notion that the individual is totally responsible for all human rights violations assumes that the violators can be identified, arrested, brought before the courts to answer for their actions and, if found guilty, punished. Again, while this procedure is familiar to many people, and is therefore 'common sense', it disregards the potential for finding structural causes of violations. To repeat, structures cannot be subjects under international law. Nor can structures be understood as independent, purposive actors with capabilities and intentions (Galtung 1994: 64). As Tomosevski has pointed out, if international human rights law seeks to identify the particular actions of particular individuals, and has little to say about the social context in which action takes place, human rights law is 'confined to redressing consequences ... without addressing the causes of human rights abuses' (Tomasevski 1993: 181). These arguments will be explored further in the discussion on international trade and human rights, which is the focus of Chapter 3.

Given these shortcomings, we might ask why do states continue to engage in the human rights debate and ratify international law on human rights? The answer to this question is found in public opinion and anxieties generated by an awareness that we live in a rapidly changing world order.

First, the technology that has been so important to transforming the global order – from one understood as a society of state to one better characterized as globalized – is widely available to those who seek to promote an awareness of the extent of human rights violations. For example, as testified by both the printed and electronic media, reports of human rights violations are almost a commonplace part of our daily experience. Moreover, the number of NGOs with an interest in human rights continues to grow, as does the authority of their reports on human rights conditions in every part of the globe. Mindful of the need to garner public opinion, governments are therefore encouraged to respond to the demand for human rights, at least in their rhetoric if not their actions.

Second, in responding to the demand for the global protection of human rights, governments seek to reinforce their own claim to legitimacy by demonstrating a positive engagement with the formal debates on human rights issues, either within the global and regional human rights regimes or at international conferences. Having done this, governments have difficulty in withdrawing from the debate when international treaties are presented for signature and ratification without tarnishing the legitimacy that concern for global human rights reinforces. Governments might adopt one of two strategies to avoid this possibility. The first is to press for the creation of non-legally binding declarations that offer moral legitimacy but not legal obligations. The second is to ensure that treaties are drafted in accordance with the principle of the 'lowest common denominator', which attracts the widest possible number of ratifications but avoids arduous obligations that might restrict future actions (Kaplan & Katzenback 1961). Both strategies offer an opportunity for governments to demonstrate concern for universal values, to garner public opinion and to reinforce traditional thinking on sovereignty and international society. In short, governments can achieve the aim of demonstrating their moral legitimacy without accepting further obligations, while simultaneously responding to their own, and the wider, public demand for human rights.

Third, governments are also aware that the obligations legitimated by international law place limitations on all signatories, including themselves. For a global hegemon, like the United States, a commitment to international law often leads to contradictions between the need to demonstrate global moral leadership and a responsibility to exercise power in the national interest or, in the age of globalization, the interests of global capital. As discussed in Chapter 1, this tension provides a recurring theme in the US's approach to universal human rights and has often led to inconsistencies in foreign policy that leave the US open to the charge of 'hypocrisy' (Chomsky 1998: 51). Attracting the moral status brought by promoting human rights while simultaneously minimizing any possible constraints on the sovereign exercise of power has preoccupied successive US presidents in recent times (Evans 1996; Muravchik 1986).

Fourth, the 'common-sense', international society tradition holds that security is concerned with the spatial exclusion of threat, the protection of the status quo and national economic stability. Anything that challenges this traditional notion of security is also seen as a challenge to the principles of sovereignty and the international system of states. Since the personal status and legitimacy of political leaders still rests upon the notion of sovereignty, most are reluctant to acknowledge the challenge of globalization and submit to the necessities of a new order. To do so would entail an admission that the problem-solving capacity of national leaders lacks potency, and would damage the status enjoyed by presidents, prime ministers and other heads of state. Entering international agreements on human rights offers an opportunity to demonstrate the explicit decision-making capacity of leaders in an age where the conditions of globalization often place limits on that capacity. Should leaders subsequently be required to take actions in fulfilment of human rights obligations, appeal to the national interest is always available as a tool for constructing a defence. The recent US ratification of the International Covenant on Civil and Political Rights (ICCPR), which was widely criticised for appearing to do something without doing anything offers an example here (Henkin 1995; Human Rights Committee 1994; Lawyers Committee for Human Rights 1992a).

Fifth, given the conditions of globalization, states face a 'veil of ignorance' that shrouds the future of world order. This takes two forms. The first follows from the issues outlined above and concerns uncertainty over the challenge that international human rights laws present to the traditional principles of the international system. The second, also discussed earlier, is concerned with the globalization of production and the increasing global reach and power of transnational corporations. The importance attached to attracting investment programmes from these corporations offers an opportunity to influence a government's policy on many issues that affect the potential for securing human rights. Zealous attention to health and safety, trade union, environmental and civil rights regulations, or a taxation system that seeks to fund social welfare, education, social housing and health programmes, are all seen as potential costs that corporations must weigh against the benefits of investing in one country rather than another. The failure to respond to these concerns reduces the chances of fulfilling the promise of economic development, bringing the threat of instability and perhaps the collapse of a government. Although less developed states are particularly exposed to these demands, global competition over investment means that most countries remain cautious over implementing any internationally agreed standard that may deter corporate investment (Evans 1997a).

Conclusion

The political energy consumed in creating international law on human rights should be evidence enough that human rights are now well established as a significant addition to the international political agenda. However, historically, international law always follows changes to social and political norms, rather than preceding them, a principle of international law well recognized by Hugo Grotius, the founder of modern international law (Grotius 1964). According to this principle, since there is no higher authority than the sovereign state, and states cannot be coerced to fulfil their international obligations, custom and the codification of existing forms of behaviour offers the only realistic opportunity of securing obedience. Since the creation of the United Nations, those with an interest in promoting human rights have tended to abandon this principle in favour of an alternative that seeks to replace custom with majority rule, paying little attention to the practice of states and ignoring the self-enforcing character of traditional thinking on international law. In this way, international law becomes orientated towards what international practice ought to be and fails to reflect the reality of current practice (Watson 1976). Although the debates on human rights cannot avoid engaging with ideas about the kind of future normative order we choose to create, an appeal to international law as a vehicle for delivering that order disregards the reality of the social, economic and political changes that are characteristic of the age of globalization and its associated forms of behaviour.

· This chapter has attempted to show that focusing so singularly on international law elevates the legal approach beyond its potential, offers a distorted view of progress in providing protection for human rights, obfuscates the structural roots of human rights violations and overlooks the inconvenient fact that international law is politically motivated. As a potential threat to traditional thinking on world order, international human rights law is particularly political. The distinction between the politics and technique of the law is rarely recognized and continues to cloud much of the debate on human rights.

The conclusion to all this is not that the law has no part to play in the protection of human rights. Rather, the conclusion is that under conditions of globalization it is not self-evident that international law, which governs relations between states, is an appropriate tool with which to protect human rights. The interstate system cannot be separated from international law: there are not two systems with international law playing the dominant role, although the literature often seems to suggest this is the case. This is inconvenient for those who adopt the international law approach to decision making for human rights, but no amount of academic or legal industry will alter the relationship. While a transnational system of law capable of regulating the behaviour of a wide range of actors, including states, transnational corporations (TNCs) and international institutions may be desirable, it does not yet exist.

Finally, the argument set out here is not simply that international law is incapable of providing protection for human rights, although its limitations are considerable, but rather that the hegemony of the international law approach acts as a further barrier to introducing the necessary social, political and economic changes to achieve such a goal. The discourse of human rights is often so fixated with existing international law, or generating new international law, that the opportunities for challenging current human rights practices, including the opportunities to press non-legal claims, are severely restricted (Stammers 1999). To focus so singularly on international law offers the illusion of orderliness that deflects attention from wide-ranging fundamental disagreements when thinking about human rights. It also deflects attention from questions to do with the continuing role of the state under conditions of globalization (Pasha & Blaney 1998). Furthermore, it deflects attention from the purpose of the human rights debate, which is to create the conditions for the realization of human security.

CHAPTER 3

The Political Economy of Human Rights

This chapter investigates the relationship between free trade and human rights under conditions of globalization. The neoliberal consensus, upon which the practices of globalization are built, resists any suggestion that moral or humanitarian issues take priority over free trade. Indeed, neoliberals argue that promoting free trade has a positive and beneficial effect on the human rights record of countries that do not comply with internationally recognized human rights standards. According to this argument, an inevitable and unregulated exchange of moral values parallels the social contact generated by the unregulated exchange of goods and services. If tyrannical governments want to enjoy the benefits of free trade, they cannot avoid the transmission of ideas that make people more aware of their rights. For neo-realists, therefore, free trade has an important educative role. It raises people's awareness to their rights and increases the demand to be treated in accordance with internationally agreed standards. In short, free trade has a potentially 'civilizing' influence on the 'uncivilized' and should be actively promoted in the name of human rights (Vincent 1986: 133–4).

If this first strand of the neoliberal argument for continuing free trade in the face of human rights violations is presented as altruistic, a second is more pragmatic. According to this second strand, disrupting free trade over human rights issues, perhaps by applying trade sanctions, has no practical value. This is for several reasons. First, under conditions of globalization, target countries have little difficulty in making alternative arrangements for the supply of essential goods, either legally or illegally. Second, to be effective, sanctions must be carefully targeted on those groups associated with tyrannical governments, rather than the wider population. The difficulties of achieving this task are immense and should not be underestimated. Third, and following from the above, the potential to 'demonize' sanctioners offers a valuable propaganda opportunity, stimulating nationalist fervour and a greater resolve to resist external coercion. Sanctions may therefore help to prolong the life of an existing tyranny rather than bring about its reform or demise. Fourth, the international political frictions generated by sanctions may have implications for security if the target state and its allies decide to resist by whatever means at their disposal. Last, at the level of domestic politics, implementing sanctions brings economic consequences for manufacturing and service industries in the sanctioner's own country and may harm the sanctioner's own interests.

Both the altruistic and pragmatic strands of the argument have been used in recent times to justify trading with those who are guilty of persistent gross violations of human rights. For example, President Carter's reluctance to apply Section 502B of the Foreign Assistance Act, which provides the power to restrict trade in security equipment with 'any country the government of which engages in a consistent pattern of gross violations of internationally recognized human rights', demonstrated that action seldom replaces rhetoric, at least not where trade with avowedly anti-communist governments was concerned (Muravchik 1986; Evans 1996: 166–70). This has remained the policy of all US presidents since Carter. The policy of 'constructive engagement' with apartheid South Africa, adopted by President Reagan, with the British prime minister, Margaret Thatcher's support, offers a further example that draws upon the neoliberal defence of free trade with human rights violators (Lawyers Committee for Human Rights 1989). More recently still, President Clinton barely hesitated before rewarding post-Tiananmen Square China with Most Favoured Nation status (Alston 1996). Finally, the failure of sanctions against Iraq may be seen as a further vindication of both the altruistic and pragmatic argument for continuing free trade (*Guardian* 1999).

Such is the success of the neoliberal consensus that '[i]n virtually all regions of the world ... there is broad acceptance of the triad of human rights, free markets and democracy as desirable [and] attainable policy objectives' (Conley & Livermore 1996). Although in achieving these aims neoliberals accept that some groups may suffer 'high transition costs', neoliberals assert that future benefits far outweigh current sacrifices (Lee 1996). The irresistible spread of free market principles on a global scale is clearly reflected in the policies of all the major international organizations, including the World Bank and the World Trade Organization (WTO). Even Michael Hansenne, the director of the International Labour Organisation (ILO), which has special responsibility for workers' rights, describes the ILO's role as 'how to find an effective means of ensuring that social progress goes hand in hand with the liberalization of trade and the globalization of the economy' (Hansenne 1996: 234).

The neoliberal defence of trading with human rights violators is therefore straightforward: if free trade then human rights, or at least the conditions necessary for the protection of human rights.

Even when the demands of globalization and international trade lead to forms of production and exchange that are the cause of violations of the right to life, security, opinion, assembly, culture and an adequate standard of living, neoliberals are reluctant to make the connection between the inconvenient facts of human rights violations and free trade (Christian Aid 1996, 1997; Human Rights Watch 1996). If neoliberals acknowledge the relationship at all, the 'high transition costs' are seen as an acceptable price to be borne stoically in the name of future generations, when all countries have fully developed economies, a goal that free trade fosters. Reports of well-documented trade-related human rights violations in many regions of the world do not seem to trouble neoliberal thinking, nor does Wallerstein's refutation of the underlying neoliberal assumption that all countries can achieve high levels of economic development or the subsequent work by Cox, Gill and other globalization theorists (Wallerstein 1983; Cox 1994; Gill 1995; see also Mittelman 1995).

The discussion here begins with a brief examination of human rights violations within the context of global trade. This is followed by some remarks on the current status of human rights and free trade under conditions of globalization. A third section offers some examples of trade-related human rights violation before drawing a conclusion.

Free Trade and Civil and Political Rights

The preceding chapters have already stressed that although the human rights debate is usually conducted in the language of philosophy and idealism, historically the norms and rules that describe the dominant view of rights in any period owe more to the struggle between competing interests (Stammers 1993). For example, the Cold War era in which the current global human rights regime emerged is often characterized as the outcome of a struggle between capitalist countries, who sought to prioritize civil and political rights, and socialist and less developed countries, who favoured economic and social rights (Evans 1996). This distinction is often criticized as simplistic and inaccurate, particularly since the two major covenants are given equal weight under international law. However, the Western, capitalist state coalition, both in the United Nations and the wider global community, has succeeded in acknowledging formal parity between the two sets of rights while simultaneously promoting only civil and political rights through rhetoric, policy and action. The most recent evidence for this was seen in the press conference given at the opening of the United Nations 2000 annual human rights assembly. Although the representatives of the world's press continually questioned Mary Robinson, the UN High Commissioner for Human Rights, on a number of high-profile abuses of civil rights, there 'was not even one question posed to Robinson about the right of the silent majority of suffering human beings ... close to half of the world population for whom life is a daily battle of survival' (Singh 2000). Philosophy may be co-opted in the interests of legitimating a particular view of rights, but politics and power determine the dominant image of rights (Stammers 1995), which in the current period marginalizes economic and social claims.

With the end of the Cold War, all resistance to the neoliberal approach to rights seems to have vanished. The now unmatched dominance of civil and political rights derives from a set of principles that emphasizes the freedom of individual action, non-interference in the private world of economics, the right to own and dispose of property, and the important principles of *laissez-faire* and free trade. The move to reduce state support for economic and social programmes in all Western countries during the last two decades, a trend that is now accepted as desirable globally, is indicative of the predominance of the neoliberal approach to rights. In the current period, legitimate human rights can only be defined as that set of rights that require government abstention from acts that violate the individual's freedom to invest time, capital and resources in processes of production and exchange (Tetrault 1988). For neoliberals, economic, social and cultural claims may be legitimate aspirations but they can never be rights.

The success of the neoliberal philosophy and practice of free trade owes much to the centrality of the individual in the human rights debate. In more recent times, collective rights are sometimes claimed, but the neoliberal consensus continues to resist all alternatives. This dispute is important but is not pursued here (Sanders 1991). As discussed in the last chapter, the corollary to the individual as the rights claimant is the individual as the perpetrator of human rights violations. Under the neoliberal consensus, just as rights reside with the individual so it follows that responsibility for violating rights also rests with the individual. Drawing on the Judeo-Christian notion of sin, those who violate human rights are wholly responsible for their own actions. Accordingly, the individual is free to act as he or she wills and must be held accountable for all their actions, including violations of human rights (Galtung 1994). It is rare to find any acknowledgement that the social, political and economic structures in which individual action takes place are of any significance when attempting to discover causation.

Although this view benefits those whose interests are best served by existing social and economic practices, because it deflects attention from structural violations (Salmi 1993), it often confuses the site of violations with the cause. Under conditions of globalization, the decisions of international financial institutions, transnational corporations (TNCs) and international organizations, which increasingly shape people's lives, are more concerned with global planning than with local consequences (Giddens 1990). Decision making becomes decoupled from the reality of people's lives. If the purpose of human rights is to guarantee the necessary freedoms for the individual fully to participate in economic life, as neoliberals argue, it is necessary to create and maintain an order that supports this goal. Human rights, human dignity and the quality of life may be desirable goals, but the application of strict free market principles is the means for achieving these ends.

The proposed Multilateral Agreement on Investment (MAI) offers a good example here. Although the process to get agreement on the MAI is currently stalled, the Organization for Economic Cooperation and Development (OECD), the international club of the world's richest countries, continues to argue that its acceptance would make a significant contribution towards completing the global programme of deregulation. The International Chamber of Commerce, the United States Council on International Business and other groups with corporate backing, undertook the first draft of the MAI, which was completed in secret. According to critics, if accepted the MAI would constitute a significant step towards creating a 'constitution of a single global economy' or 'a bill of rights and freedoms for transnational corporations ... a declaration of corporate rule' (Kothari 1998). This 'constitution' would further restrict state powers to formulate independent policy and curtail the rights of peoples to enjoy the benefits of their natural resources. The practice of imposing human rights-related investment conditions, such as employing local labour, providing education and training and making a contribution to the local economy, would be outlawed under the MAI. Similarly, anti-discrimination measures would be outlawed, including food subsidies, regulation of land speculation, agrarian reform, government-sponsored health programmes and environmental controls. In short, critics argue that the MAI represents a major step in the attempt to promote free trade that serves the interests of international investors and corporations, without regard for the rights of workers, communities and the environment.

A central feature of the dominant neoliberal view of rights is the presumption that civil and political rights are qualitatively and significantly different from economic and social rights. In recent times it has become commonplace to see this distinction referred to as one between 'negative' (civil and political) and 'positive' (economic and social) rights. According to this argument, negative rights require people to refrain from doing anything that impairs the freedoms of others, while positive rights require others to provide the material means of life to those unable to provide for themselves – at a minimum, food, clean water, shelter and clothing (Plant 1993). In other words, the protection of negative rights demands restraint while the protection of positive rights demands action. By promoting negative claims as the only truly universal human rights, which obliges the individual to refrain from acts that violate others' freedoms, structural causes are rendered invisible. Given that the individual cannot be held responsible for the prevailing economic, social and political context in which action takes place, all actions that conform to the prevailing neoliberal orthodoxy are understood as legitimate. If the prevailing orthodoxy permits economic transactions with human rights consequences, the individual cannot be held responsible (Chomsky 1998). Accordingly, through prioritizing negative rights, neoliberals provide a defence against critics who see the causes of many human rights violations as embedded in the structures of the global economic order.

The defence of negative claims as the limits of universal human rights rests upon several assumptions. First, negative rights can be guaranteed through the simple expedient of passing national laws that guarantee restraint. Negative rights are therefore cost free in as far as they require forebearance rather than the redistribution of resources. Second, since all rights are claimed against the state, and positive rights depend upon the level of economic development a country has achieved, setting any universal standards for economic and social rights is impossible. To attempt to do so would demand that some countries acknowledge rights that they could not realistically deliver. Third, economic and social claims, like the right to a certain standard of living, are culturally determined. To talk of a universal right to holidays with pay (Universal Declaration of Human Rights (UDHR) Art. 24), for example, makes no sense in societies where the concept of holidays or pay has no meaning. Fourth, the correlative duty of forebearance clearly rests with all members of society when negative rights are claimed but this is not so for positive rights. Indeed, the attempt to impose a duty on wealthy countries to fulfil positive rights may conflict with negative freedoms, particularly those associated with economic activity, including free market practices and the freedom to own and dispose of property. Last, since the right to life is the most basic universal right from which all other claims derive, and the right to life is one of forebearance, negative rights must be ranked above positive rights (Cranston 1973, 1983).

At first sight these arguments appear compelling. If individuals, corporations and international organizations conform to the prevailing norms of conduct, and the only truly universal human rights are negative claims, then no blame can be levelled at those who take advantage of prevailing practices, regardless of the human rights consequences. Put another way, if the principles of free trade are supported by negative freedoms, and the legitimate investment strategies of TNCs leads to the displacement of people, loss of livelihoods or the destruction of traditional communities, no blame can be apportioned for human rights violations.

In seeking a reply to this view, it is worth returning to the work of Henry Shue, undertaken many years before the word 'globalization' entered the language. Shue states that 'neither rights to physical security nor rights to subsistence fit neatly into their assigned sides of the simplistic positive/negative dichotomy', an assertion which remains at the centre of the neoliberal consensus on rights (Shue 1980: 37). For Shue, basic rights to food and shelter are more positive than neoliberals claim and physical security rights are more negative. If this is so, then the claim that civil and political rights must take priority over economic and social cannot be easily sustained. More important, if Shue's claim is correct, it may be possible to apportion blame and impose duties on those who pursue so-called 'negative' rights that lead to human rights consequences.

In opposition to a neoliberal view, Shue begins by arguing that people cannot enjoy the full range of internationally agreed human rights without first securing certain basic rights. These are the rights to life, security and subsistence. Shue argues that none of these are wholly negative or wholly positive claims. For example, while in some cases understanding physical security as a negative right is correct, in the sense that all members of society undertake a duty not to violate others' rights, this is only a partial description of what we understand by a human right. According to Shue, even neoliberals accept that in human rights talk the right to security infers a commitment not merely to forebearance but to make arrangements to *protect* those whose rights are threatened and to *avoid* taking any action that leads to violations. The demand for civil and political rights is 'not normally a demand simply to be left alone, but a demand to be protected against harm ... It is a demand for positive action ... a demand for social guarantees against at least the standard threats' (Shue 1980: 39). Furthermore, the means to guaranteeing negative rights is positive action, including the creation and maintenance of a legislature, police, a legal system, courts, prisons and taxation to fund these measures. Neoliberal arguments that negative rights are cost-free overlooks this aspect of negative rights.

Similarly, it is misleading to label subsistence rights as exclusively positive claims. Just as accepting the negative duty of forebearance can satisfy the right to physical security, accepting a negative duty not to engage in practices that frustrate people's endeavours to provide for themselves can satisfy subsistence rights. Expressed cogently by Shue:

> All that is sometimes necessary is to protect the persons whose subsistence is threatened from the individuals and institutions that will otherwise intentionally or unintentionally harm them. A demand for a right to subsistence may involve not a demand to be provided with grants of commodities but merely a demand to be provided some opportunity for supporting oneself. The request is not to be supported but to be allowed to be self-supporting on the basis of one's own hard work. (Shue 1980: 40)

Thus, if TNCs use the free market to invest in ways that deprive people of the means of subsistence, or if the WTO, the North American Free Trade Agreement (NAFTA) and the EU implement free trade rules, practices and procedures that deprive people of the means to achieve subsistence for themselves, this is also a denial of human rights. Consequently, 'those who deny rights can have no complaint when the denial ... is resisted' (Shue 1980: 14). In this view of negative and positive rights, international institutions, the state and its agents and TNCs have a duty not to engage in practices, including trade practices, that indirectly lead to human rights violations, not merely those actions for which they have direct responsibility (Addo 1987).

Shue does not deny that on occasion circumstances may demand a redistribution of resources from the wealthy to those unable to provide the basic needs of life for themselves. However, he concludes that if rights are never wholly negative or positive then correlative duties cannot be wholly negative or positive. For example, the correlative duties associated with the right to life must include a duty to *avoid* harm (negative), a duty to *protect* from harm (negative/positive) and a duty to *aid* those threatened (positive). Similarly, the right to subsistence includes a duty to *avoid* taking action that deprives others of the means of subsistence, a duty to *protect* others, whose only means of subsistence is threatened, and a duty to *aid* those unable to provide for their own subsistence. For Shue, the means to achieving basic subsistence security

> ... could be controlled by some combination of the mere restraint of second parties and the maintenance of protective

institutions by first and third parties, just as the standard threats that deprive people of their physical security could be controlled by restraint and protection from non-restraint. (Shue 1980: 41)

Shue's interest is in exposing the structural practices that are the cause of many human rights violations, practices that the neoliberal consensus has elevated to the status of 'common-sense' habits that are part of a natural, normal and rational approach to modern life (Muzaffar 1995). It is these 'common-sense' practices that provide the rationale for denying responsibility for human rights violations and a means for international organizations, states and TNCs to avoid all criticism of their own decisions and actions.

Shue's analysis offers a considerable challenge to the neoliberal consensus in the context of globalization, the free market and the dominant conception of universal human rights. In particular, Shue confronts the rules and practices of trade, as described by the WTO, NAFTA, the EU and other international organizations concerned with trade relations. He also challenges TNCs that seek to defend their decisions with the claim that their obligations extend only to negative responsibilities. However, despite Shue, in the age of globalization, the dominant neoliberal view of trade and human rights shows few signs of change.

Globalization, Free Trade and Human Rights

Before looking at some examples of situations where government and TNC activity is inextricably linked to human rights violations, this section looks at the status of human rights under the emerging global free trade system. It remains common practice to prioritize trade issues over those of human rights, although the rhetoric often suggests otherwise. Globalization has strengthened the conviction of many commentators that the current world order values human life only for its contribution towards ever greater economic growth and the continued expansion of global capital (Gill 1995; Watkins 1996). Making this point, Noam Chomsky has observed that although the deregulation of global markets might be convenient for those who see 'profit for investors as the supreme human value, to which all else must be subordinated', such that '[h]uman life has value as far as it contributes to this end' (Chomsky 1994: 270–1), it leaves little room for developing a strategy for the protection of human rights. Similarly, as Michael Lewis has observed, while Secretary of State Madeleine Albright continues to speak in the language of human rights and values, '[t]he world would be more true to itself if the American embassies were sold off to American investment banks as foreign branch offices' (Lewis 1998).

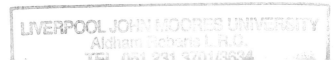

This is not to suggest that the discourse on universal human rights is of no further interest to the neoliberal consensus. On the contrary, the defence of negative rights, including the right freely to own and dispose of property, promotes the accumulation of capital to the detriment of policies that could have benefited the poor through education, health and social programmes. The promotion of negative freedoms in support of free market principles is seen in the greater attention given to international law on trade, property and finance, compared to that concerned with humanitarian issues (Chomsky 1994). It is also reflected in the move towards creating powerful international organizations, like the WTO, with responsibility for protecting the rights and freedoms of capital in global trade relations. The development of this new legal order, to which states increasingly submit, supports the arguments of globalization theory that the image of the autonomous, decision-making state no longer reflects reality, making the distinction between internal and external authority less clear. As expressed by one scholar, 'it becomes progressively more difficult to demonstrate the primacy of domestic law, which is arguably one of the cardinal premises of state sovereignty' (Camilleri 1990: 22).

This leads to the argument, previously encountered in Chapter 2, that the image of the state as the central actor engaged in all aspects of international political life, and the primary defender of universal human rights, cannot be sustained. According to globalization theory, the state has assumed a new role as a unit for creating and maintaining the structures necessary to sustain an efficient global economy (Panitch 1995). However, the transformation of state power is not evenly distributed over all international issues, but is more concentrated on economic planning and trade. Transnational forces replace the authority of the state because the state 'aggregates the energies and synergy of human activity at a political and territorial level that does not correspond to evolving flows of labour, capital and technology' (Mittelman 1997: 101). The potential for conflict within the new global order is fomented when leaders attempt to contest the reality of globalization by pursuing economic nationalism.

This raises important questions about both human rights and democracy, two concepts that neoliberals promote as symbiotic (Carothers 1994). The emerging global economy represents a move to ever greater ideological homogeneity, which places economic growth at the top of the political agenda. Homogeneity requires that all national economies adjust to the exigencies of global strategic planning and management. Conformity is guaranteed by international organization, such as the WTO, which has the authority to implement rules without regard for the national interest, human dignity or human rights. Thus, critics argue that while the WTO may bring order and predictability by ensuring conformity with trade rules, which promotes the interests of transnational corporations and global finance, it also 'represents another stake in the heart of the idea that governments can direct economies' (George 1999: 21, quoting the *Wall Street Journal*). Although in previous periods governments could expect to implement national economic strategies, as corporations move increasingly to global systems of production, finance and investment, state intervention in the interest of citizens' rights or human rights becomes less possible. Chapter 4 looks at the relationship between human rights and democracy in greater detail.

The activity of TNCs without clear national loyalties or identities further weakens the relationship between government and the national economy. TNCs make investment and production decisions within a global context in order to maximize profit, not in a national context, which might include a concern for human rights. The global free market in which these corporations operate is not therefore concerned with the traditional boundaries provided by the state. While in the past the state could hope to manage its own national economy to provide minimal social welfare through fiscal and interventionist policies, import barriers and export subsidies, today a global, 24-hour market operates that pays no homage to national economic planning (Held & McGrew 1993: 270–1).

Over the past two decades TNCs have consolidated their economic power base. Between 1980 and 1992 the annual sales of TNCs doubled ($2.4 to $5.5 trillion), and the annual sales of many are now greater than the GDP of some states. For example, in 1997, General Motors' world-wide sales ($164 billion, approximately one-third of which was in foreign sales) exceeded the GDP of Thailand ($154 billion), Norway ($153 billion), Poland ($136 billion) and Malaysia ($98 billion) (UNDP 1999). Coupled with new technology that allows rapid movements of finance and capital, TNCs use their economic power to gain the most favourable conditions for their activities. Locked into an ideology of modernity, economic growth and development, states become involved in a 'Dutch auction', where countries bid against each other to offer the lowest levels of environmental, labour and human rights regulation, in the hope of attracting TNC investment. John Carlin's contention that 'on the one hand, multinationals promote the dismantling of government controls [while] on the other, they are busy forging pacts to manage trade privately', free of democratic control and accountability, captures much of the activity of TNCs under globalization (Carlin 1998; see also Christian Aid 1999). One unforeseen consequence of adopting strategies intended to maximize economic growth in the interests of TNCs is growing inequality, and in some countries an 'absolute decline in real income of the bottom forty to sixty percent of families' (Beitz 1983). Thus, for economic and social rights the conclusion is that 'development processes (trade agreements, national economic development strategies, and so forth), individuals, organisations (multilateral lenders, multinational and national corporations), and governments, all deny human rights' (Johnston & Button 1994: 213; see also UNDP 1996).

The consequences of the 'Dutch auction' are severest in those countries that have experienced rapid economic expansion, where the price for maintaining a semblance of economic independence is the acceptance of risk. In these countries, rights are threatened because, as Waters points out, 'safety regulations are weak and unenforced and populations are insufficiently literate to be aware of the risks they run even where they have a choice about whether to be engaged in the risky endeavour of, say, spreading fertilizers and pesticides by hand' (Waters 1995: 61). These risks are of little concern to transnational corporations, since managers are aware that their investment power is sufficient to persuade governments to overlook potential dangers. Moreover, corporate managers are also aware that their resources are sufficiently great to defend against any legal action that may follow an industrial accident or compensation claims for bad health. Many governments of emerging economies also reject the suggestion that they should minimize these risks, arguing, for example, that the enforcement of labour standards as a condition for investment smacks of protectionism and an attempt to 'overcome the comparative advantage of low-wage developing countries' (WTO Singapore Ministerial Declaration 1998).

While the development of a global economy is not a new phenomenon (Hirst & Thompson 1996), access to new technology, particularly information technology, accelerates processes of social inclusion and exclusion. New technology enables production to be planned and financed on a global scale. According to neoliberals, the use of technology brings benefits to all members of society, although they rarely explain the mechanism by which this is achieved (Ropke 1991: 13; Lee 1996; ILO 1996). Furthermore, there is the presumption that technology is an autonomous force, beyond social control and the prevailing social and political contexts in which it emerges (Berting 1993). This adds further weight to the neoliberal notion of personal responsibility in the field of human rights, since no individual or group can be held responsible for violations where technological development is seen as external to social relations.

An alternative view rejects the characterization of technology as autonomous, neutral and value free. In this view, the decision-making and organizational practices of particular interests determine which technologies are developed, introduced or abandoned, and to what purposes and uses a particular new technology will be put. There might be a 'trade-off' between human rights and the technologies that drive globalization and economic development, but this is a political choice (Donnelly 1989b), independent of the technology itself. If human rights violations occur as a result of these choices, then those responsible should not seek absolution on the grounds that technological 'progress' is in some way inevitable, irreversible and irresistible, contrary to President Clinton's recent WTO speech claiming that '[g]lobalization is not a political choice – it is a fact' (WTO, 18 May 1998).

The success of the formal global human rights regime developed at the United Nations depends upon the relationship between rights, national democracy and domestic law (UDHR Art. 21:1; International Covenant on Civil and Political Rights (ICCPR) Art. 25). Globalization, including the pursuit of free trade, suggests that national democratic institutions are becoming weaker and, consequently, the ability of governments to implement national law to resist trade-related violations of human rights is rendered less effective. On the one hand, the formal regime stresses the importance of the state as the central agent for implementing universal human rights, while on the other the state is losing its capacity to fulfil its obligations. This is particularly evident in the activities of global trade, where the rules and practices enforced by the WTO and regional trading blocs are afforded greater authority than national decision-making processes. Given that the authority of the state has less significance in important areas of economic life, it becomes more difficult for states to take human rights seriously. Furthermore, the 'common sense' of achieving ever greater levels of economic growth and development means that states are inclined to overlook human rights issues in favour of economic interests.

Trade-related Violations of Human Rights

Following the above examination of the neoliberal approach to human rights and globalization, examining violations of human rights as the outcome of current free trade practices is now possible. These violations are not restricted to economic and social rights alone, but also include violations of civil and political rights. The 'Dutch auction' referred to above, where low standards act as a magnet for TNC and foreign investment (Watkins 1996), leads to the destruction of cultural life, degrades the environment, leaves people without the means to provide for their own subsistence and creates physical and mental health problems that tear communities and families apart. Moreover, those who attempt to counter these consequences, perhaps by organizing a trade union or resistance group, are often subjected to actual violence or the threat of violence for daring to express a contrary view about their own and their community's future. Such violence is often officially, if covertly, sanctioned (Salmi 1993).

Although in recent times human rights talk has included some discussion of exercising a duty to avoid violating others' rights, this is always within a framework that venerates trade. For the director-general of the ILO, the WTO is the 'senior partner' in a process that seeks to steer a path between the necessities of liberalization and workers' rights (Hansenne 1996). This approach to trade and human rights seems to overlook the issues raised above. In particular, it ignores important questions about free trade as the cause of human rights violations and current methods for protecting rights. So long as corporate decision makers continue to argue that their responsibility is to shareholders, not the public at large or even their own workforce, the opportunity to instil a sense of duty in human rights issues seems unlikely. The standard response of corporate decision makers is that if there is a demand for imposing a duty of social responsibility upon TNCs then it is up to governments, through international organizations and inter-national law, to implement procedures that clarify exactly what those duties are.

The objections to this approach should be obvious from the analysis offered above. First, given the conditions of globalization, particularly the declining ability of the state to regulate transna-tional actors, the argument that corporations will accept duties only in response to international law seems more like an exercise in obfuscation than a genuine concern to create rules for human rights. As one critic has observed:

> A system based on individual freedom, self-regulation and 'Darwinian' competition and survival of the fittest will not suddenly turn around and, by and of itself, beg to be regulated. The system's chief beneficiaries cannot be expected or, under present circumstances, forced to act against their own immediate interests, against the very principles of profit and self-advantage upon which the free market and their own success are founded. To imagine that these beneficiaries might, in large or even significant numbers, recognise in time the need for external

regulation is to deny all known laws of human behaviour. This contradiction must be underscored and faced. (George 1999: 29)

Second, the recent history of TNC lobbying suggests a close relationship between governments, international organizations and corporations, which does not give confidence about creating any regulatory regime for overseeing a duty to avoid human rights violations (Chatterjee & Finger 1994). This close relationship is seen in the appointment of past Chairs of the GATT and the WTO to the boards of multinational corporations and industrial and financial lobbying organizations. Christian Aid reports, for example, that Arther Dunkel, Chair of GATT from 1980 to 1993, now chairs the Working Group on Trade and Investment for the International Chamber of Commerce and is on the board of Nestlé. His successor, Peter Sutherland, is reported to be involved in the lobbying group the European Roundtable of Industrialists, and is also Chair of BP and an associate of Goldman Sachs. Renato Ruggerio, director-general of the WTO from 1995 to 1999, 'immediately found a place on the board of the Italian petroleum company ENI' (Christian Aid 1999). Furthermore, at the bilateral level, TNCs regularly 'play one government off against another and choose to invest only where they win the greatest concession' (UNRISD (United Nations Research Institute for Social Development) 1995: 160).

Third, despite the widely acknowledged benefits that the WTO brings to TNCs, and their growing importance within the global political economy, the Uruguay Round did not see fit to mention TNCs at its completion (UNRISD 1995), although the WTO rules give support for extending the rights of TNCs while limiting further the regulatory powers of the state (LeQuesne 1996: 17–18). The trade rules for restricting government action to control trade-related investment measures (TRIMS) is, perhaps, the most significant of these powers. Finally, a further indication of the success of big business and finance to remain free of any human rights duty imposed by the wider international community is the failure of the United Nations to adopt a code of conduct for TNC activities. The United Nations abandoned this possibility in 1994 following disputes between industrialized countries, less developed countries and international business interests (Watkins 1996).

This raises several important questions concerning the emerging new world order based on neoliberal values of free trade. When does a government's economic policy go beyond the legitimate purpose of government, which is to protect the rights, security, liberty and economic well-being of its people? How should a government react when resistance to trade-related development projects is encountered? Should governments continue to protect the rights of corporations engaged in trade-related development projects, which might mean using the police and military to suppress peaceful resistance, or are the people's rights to freedom of thought, expression and association paramount? In a globalized world, where the power of the state to control important areas of domestic life is in decline, should people expect greater support and accountability from the complex of international organizations that make decisions with global consequences? These questions, which all concern democracy, human rights, the changing nature of citizenship and the limits of freedom under conditions of globalization, are pressing but remain unanswered (Tatum 1996; Held 1995).

What follows here is a selection of examples where current trade practices lead to human rights violations. They demonstrate that the 'common-sense' approach to free trade adopted by all governments, corporations and international organizations, is intolerant of any alternative world-view. When alternatives are expressed, and individuals and groups take action in defence of their economic, social, civil and political claims, governments and corporations routinely violate human rights. The word 'routinely' is not out of place here if we accept the description of killings of peasant leaders as 'traditional abuses', a phrase used by Mariclare Acosta, President of the Mexican Commission for the Defense of Human Rights (Acosta 1992: 82). These 'traditional abuses' are a common response when those whose lives are directly affected by globalization dare to challenge the 'prevailing orthodoxy' on free trade (Chomsky 1998; see also Thomas 1998). The former president of Ecuador Abdala Bacaram's assertion that '[i]f oil workers seek to halt the production of basic and strategic services such as oil, I will personally witness the police and the armed forces giving them a thrashing to make them return to work' is perhaps more blunt than most; however, it is not so far removed from the attitude of many governments and corporations (Ganesan 1998). The following examples are representative and do not form anything like a comprehensive list. Many similar examples could have been chosen.

The damaging effects of trade on civil and economic rights, and the failure to accept a duty to avoid violations, is seen most vividly in commercial prawn farming. Driven by a narrow economic definition of growth and development, many less developed countries have encouraged commercial prawn farming ventures without regard for social and environmental consequences. Concerned by growing Third World debt, the World Bank and other international financial institutions have supported any venture that promises to improve a country's balance of payments by increasing exports. Commercial prawn farming has the added advantage that it brings high returns on low levels of investment and technology. This is particularly attractive to private investors with an eye on making enormous profits in the short term.

The farming method involves the construction of saline ponds, ranging in size from a half-hectare to five hectares. The optimum conditions for prawn cultivation are maintained in a number of ways: continuously pumping water, and adding chemicals to control acidity and alkalinity, fertilizers for growth, antibiotics to control disease and other chemicals to combat parasites. The timescale from stocking the ponds with seedling prawns to harvest is usually four months, allowing companies to take three crops a year. One crop is often sufficient to cover investment costs (Christian Aid 1996). While the demand for prawns continues to increase in wealthy industrialized countries, commercial prawn farming will remain an important source of foreign exchange for many Asian and Latin American countries.

While this sounds like good news to those who understand growth and development in strictly economic terms, the human rights consequences are considerable. Often, producers site prawn farms on what the government classifies as 'waste land' considered as unsuitable for any other use. However, these sites are often common lands, representing a valuable resource for local communities and providing the only available access to pasture, fuel-wood and other necessities to sustain life. Christian Aid reports that in some cases prawn farming has taken over land previously used for producing locally marketed foods. In other cases, prawn farm sites obstruct access to beaches, which had previously supported a local fishing community. Similarly, the construction of ponds can obstruct the natural flow of water and cause flooding in villages, land erosion and the salination of soil. Producers often pump waste water onto adjacent lands, polluting the soil with a cocktail of additives used in prawn production. Although many of these practices are illegal, 'governments have ignored violations of ... laws in their enthusiasm for promoting prawn farms' (Christian Aid 1996: 14–15). The outcome is that people are forced from the land that provides subsistence and their traditional way of life disintegrates, violating economic and cultural rights that are protected under international law.

Furthermore, prawn farming often leads to violations of civil and political rights. Prawn farmers are prone to issuing threats if local people refuse to leave properties that occupy potential prawn farm sites (Watkins 1996). If threats fail, the authorities have attacked villages and burned down houses. In one such incident reported by Christian Aid:

... villagers staged a large rally ... to oppose the construction of a new prawn farm ... On the same day pro-prawn farm landowners and thugs hired by the prawn companies set fire to 33 houses in the village and beat up two women. There was also an altercation ... which the police became involved in. Villagers say that not only did the police refuse to register a case against the landowners and thugs, but the next day they came ... and arrested 28 [local] people. (Christian Aid 1996: 18–19)

Mexico's Maquiladora sector offers a further example. The Maquiladora produces $29 billion in export earnings and provides employment for more than 500,000 people from the poorest, least experienced and least educated groups in society. Human rights violations are reported in many parts of the sector, particularly in relation to attempts to establish free trade unions (Herrmann 1993; Johnston & Button 1994). Where possible, the corporations operating in the Maquiladora prefer to employ women, ostensibly because of their greater dexterity and commitment to the job. Labour activists dispute this, however, arguing that employers view women as less informed about their rights, less radical than men, more tolerant of substandard working conditions and less likely to engage in political or trade union activism (McDonald 1999: 56).

The example offered here concerns discrimination against women based on pregnancy. Human Rights Watch confirms that applicants for jobs are routinely subjected to pregnancy tests before being hired. In some cases employers questioned women about their sexual activities, when they last menstruated and whether they used contraception. If women do become pregnant, managers often attempt to force then to resign, using several methods intended to intimidate, including picking on every conceivable error in the quality of work, no matter how trivial; providing substandard machines with no capacity to achieve bonus payment targets; refusing to allow time off to attend the doctor, and transferring the women to heavier, more physically demanding work usually considered inappropriate for pregnant women.

Although Mexican labour law forbids such discrimination, the government frequently tolerates the practices described above. Human Right Watch concluded that pregnancy-based discrimination against women persists because of a 'confluence of interests and needs: the economic interests of Maquiladora operators to keep their operating cost as low as possible, government interest in attracting and keeping foreign investment, and women's desperation to keep jobs' (HRW 1996: 7). Neither the corporations nor the government seem interested in responding to internationally recognized prohibitions on pregnancy-based discrimination. Under the ICCPR (Art. 26), all people are entitled to equal treatment before the law regardless of sex. The Convention on the Elimination of All Forms of Discrimination Against Women (CEDAW) (Art. 2) condemns all forms of discrimination against women, particularly in the field of employment (Art. 11:1). Discriminatory pregnancy-based practices are also a violation of the right to privacy (ICCPR Art. 17; UDHR Art. 12) and the right to decide freely the number and spacing of children (CEDAW Art. 16:1).

A further example can be seen where Maquiladora workers struggled to establish free trade unions, independent of the government-backed Confederation of Mexican Workers (CMW). In 1989, for example, workers at the Ford plant in Hermoville organized a hunger strike in support of their demand for democratic elections to the CMW. In response, Ford began to fire workers and blacklist those involved in the action, but protests continued. Of a total of 3,800 workers, Ford dismissed 3,050 before the organizers called off the action (Johnston & Button 1994).

Another example concerns the activities of Shell Oil in the Ogoni region of Nigeria. Human Rights Watch reports that at the end of October 1990, Shell requested police assistance at a peaceful demonstration against the continued destruction of tribal lands as a direct result of oil operations. Beatings, teargas attacks and indiscriminate shootings followed, resulting in the deaths of 80 people and the wrecking of 495 homes. On another occasion one of Shell's contractors, Willbros, bulldozed crops in preparation for construction work. When local people protested, Willbros called in government troops who opened fire to disperse the demonstrators. Willbros defended its right to proceed with the construction, on the grounds that all the necessary formal procedures were adhered to, although the popular Movement for the Protection of the Ogoni People was not invited to take part in the negotiations that sanctioned the contract (HRW 1995).

Although Shell has claimed that the company's contact with Nigerian security forces was minimal, a government official admitted to Human Rights Watch that regular contact was made with the Director of Rivers State Security, Lieutenant Colonel Paul Okuntimo. According to one company official, Okuntimo was a 'savage soldier', known for his brutality, who saw his role as making 'the area safe for the oil companies' (HRW 1995: 38).

Following a stormy shareholder meeting in the summer of 1997, at which shareholders called for greater openness and social responsibility, Shell has recently announced its intention to publish an annual audit of social accountability. With the aim of placing Shell as the forefront of social corporate reporting, the report will 'illustrate day-to-day practice' against a set of operating principles published last year, according to Tom Delfgaauw, the manager of Shell's social accountability unit (Crow 1998). It remains to be seen whether this approach to taking human rights seriously proves beneficial. Broad statements of intent are easier to achieve than a change in corporate culture or the actions necessary to ensure that human rights policies are enforced. However, many human rights NGOs see this as an important breakthrough, which deserves encouragement.

Another example concerns new port facilities, placing it conspicuously at the centre of all trade issues. The developers, P&O, are proposing to construct a port, reportedly eight times the size of Liverpool, in Dahanu, the home of one of India's few remaining tribal peoples, the Warlis. Although at the time of writing, P&O had not reached a final decision to go ahead with the project, the government of Maharashtra is on record as determined to see the new port completed. The chief minister of Maharashtra believes that the construction will bring much needed jobs to the area and regenerate the economy. P&O intends that the proposed port relieves the congestion at Bombay, where delays in turning ships around are already costly.

However, an unpublished report commissioned by P&O concludes that 'the port will destroy the Warlis way of life' (Burrell 1998). In a survey undertaken by the report's authors, 70 per cent of the Warlis are opposed to the port, with only 11 per cent in favour. Contrary to the government of Maharashtra's claim that the port will bring lasting economic benefits, the authors conclude that there is little evidence of this. Indeed, the authors report that 'the sustainable use of natural resources has created a flourishing economy', which is 'self-sufficient and rooted in the natural wealth of the region'. If P&O does go ahead with the construction, the local economy will be destroyed and the human rights impact extensive.

The final example concerns the sports goods industry. The annual average export value of Indian sports goods, which produces among other items baseballs, footballs, cricket equipment, volleyballs and boxing gloves, rose by an average of 21 per cent during the 1990s. Most of these items are produced for well-known brand names, who market them throughout the world. Although no reliable official statistics exist, Christian Aid estimates that of the 300,000 workers engaged in the industry, some 25,000 to 30,000 are children, working either with their families or in small stitching centres. Some children, aged between 10 and 11 years, work five or six hours a day for as little as 12 pence per football, which produces an effective hourly rate of six pence. In addition, 'tanneries supplying leather to the industry's main exporters also employ children, exposing them to hazardous chemicals.' Children and teenage apprentices working in factories or small workshops are routinely paid a fraction of the adult minimum wage. In addition to poor pay, some adult workers are denied union rights, sick pay and access to provident funds and insurance schemes. It is common practice to fire and rehire workers 'to avoid granting the permanent rights due by law to those employed continuously for more than 200 days' (Christian Aid 1997).

The Constitution of India permits children to work in family-run industries, in agriculture and in small-scale manufacturing units that do not use hazardous processes. The 1948 Factories Act does, however, ban employers from hiring child labour in specific industries, including leather tanning. While these legal constraints offer some protection to children, child labour law is selectively implemented at best and attracts no resources for implementation at worst. Employers routinely employ children in small units, a practice explicitly excluded from regulation under labour law. For this and other technical reasons, the Child Labour Act does not cover 92 per cent of children. Where inspection programmes operate, the resources are inadequate and corruption among inspectors is widespread.

Although the work of children often makes an important contribution to the economic survival of the family, particularly in the poorest sectors of society, the International Labour Organisation (ILO) makes a distinction between child work and child labour (ILO Minimum Age Convention, No. 138). Work includes those tasks that are not onerous and those that teach a trade or help support the family economy. Labour, on the other hand, involves prolonged hard toil, which interferes with a child's schooling, damages a child's physical and mental development, hinders their future prospects and depresses wages locally. The use of children in the production of sports goods for export does not represent the worst case of child exploitation for profit. Indeed, according to Christian Aid, campaigners have had some success in persuading employers to alter their employment policies and reduce their dependency on child labour. However, it does provide a further example where the development of globally managed production and investment encourages practices that lead to human rights violations, in this case the rights of the child.

Conclusion

The above examples show how many internationally recognized human rights are violated in the cause of trade. People who stand in the way of trade-related business 'routinely' lose the right to self-determination and to 'freely pursue their economic, social and cultural development' (International Convenant on Economic, Social and Cultural Rights (ICECSR) Art. 1:1). In some cases, local resistance to trade-related development projects lead to the violation of the right to 'life, liberty and the security of the person' (UDHR Art. 3). The right to form and join trade unions 'for the promotion and protection of ... economic and social interests' (ICESCR Art. 8), is also a target for oppressive measures. The right to subsistence is violated when people are excluded from their traditional means of feeding, clothing and housing themselves (ICESCR Art. 11). The special protection afforded to women under CEDAW seems to attract little respect when there is a need for low-paid obedient workers engaged in the production of export goods.

Since the economic, social and cultural violations described above are 'the products of specific human decisions permitted by the presence of specific social institutions and the absence of others' (Shue 1980: 44), it is reasonable to look towards established structures and processes for causation. In other words, corporations, financial institutions, governments and international organizations are responsible for violations through their decision-making processes, just as any perpetrator of human rights violations is responsible. Under the current conditions of globalization, this is not a widely held view.

Although there is much talk about Social Charters for addressing the labour, social and economic consequences of trade, experience of such measures indicates that the powerful would gain the most. If the standards set by a Social Charter could only be met by wealthy developed countries, a Charter could be used as a tool for exclusionary practices that lead to even greater levels of deprivation. Some have suggested that the way forward is to abandon the idea of rights as a focus for action and to replace it with an ethic of care. Such a shift, it is argued, requires judgements to be made about needs, conflicting needs and the strategies adopted for achieving ends, an approach that places an obligation on TNCs, banks and governments to take account of both public and private needs (Robinson 1998).

However, so long as human rights talk remains of use to the neoliberal consensus, legitimating some actions and outlawing others, it seems likely that structural causes of violations will be ignored.

CHAPTER 4

Globalization, Democracy and Human Rights

The previous chapters have stressed the tension between universal claims and those of sovereignty. If everyone claims human rights, 'and everyone equally, by virtue of their very humanity' (Vincent 1986: 13), then sustaining a definition of sovereignty that includes non-intervention, domestic jurisdiction, self-determination and non-interference in the internal life of the nation, is no simple task. However, with the end of the Cold War, the globalization of the state and the potential for greater levels of communication facilitated by the rapid spread of information technology, many came to believe that the prospects for protecting human rights were never better. For some commentators, such a conclusion was further supported by the growing acceptance of liberal democracy as the best, indeed the only legitimate, form of government, since liberal democracy and human rights are understood as two sides of the same coin (Carothers 1994). This view was articulated by the then United Nations Secretary-General Boutros Boutros-Ghali, when he argued that 'democracy is a thread which runs through all the work of the Organization' and that 'human rights, equal rights and government under law are important attributes of democracy' (Fox & Nolte 1995: 5).

The simple equation 'if democracy then human rights' is not, however, as self-evident as might appear at first sight. Before examining the reasons for treating the assumed relationship between human rights and democracy with caution, something should be said about the idea of democracy at the beginning of the twenty-first century. Although there are distinctive versions of liberalism, and therefore of liberal democracy, each of which provides a different approach to agency, autonomy and rights, talk of democracy in the post-Cold War era usually refers to some form of representative democracy, such as that claimed to have triumphed over socialist alternatives. Four important general assumptions flow from this widely held view of democracy, which are important to our discussion.

The first assumption is that the territorial state is the appropriate community for democratization (Held 1992; Hindess 1999). The territorial state is the basic unit that defines the limits of democracy, insiders from outsiders and citizens from non-citizens. This is not to suggest all people living within a particular democratic state share the rights associated with citizenship equally: indeed, in all liberal democracies the constitution makes some provision to exclude some categories of people from full participation, for example, children, aliens, criminals, the insane. However, at the millennium, the generally held assumption is that the concept of liberal democracy is tied to the idea of a self-governing community, a community of citizens defined by national sovereignty, the territorial nation-state, self-determination and domestic jurisdiction. This view is so entrenched that most commentators would agree that 'political theory has made a profound connection between democracy and the nation-state' (Clark 1999: 147), which international theory and practice reinforce, placing democracy squarely within the domestic sphere.

The second assumption places the principle of accountability at the centre of all forms of liberal democracy. Upholding important civil freedoms secures the guarantee of this principle, including the freedom of speech, assembly and the press. Accountability is further guaranteed through the practice of holding periodic elections to a representative assembly, a practice that is widely understood as the single most important requirement for a government to claim democratic credentials. According to this assumption, the constitution of a democratically elected representative assembly, possessing both the powers to approve all taxation and legislation and the capability to scrutinize the actions of the executive branch of government, provides the basic building block upon which all other attributes of democracy rest. As the central institution concerned with accountability, the responsibilities of a representative assembly concerns harmonizing popular demands and political equality with the demands of globalization, which provides the context in which the modern liberal democratic state operates (Beetham 1992).

The third assumption is that democratic states continue to exercise a high degree of autonomy, including the capabilities to pursue policies that further the interests of the people. Citizens have an expectation that governments can, in fact, fulfil the aims and objectives of the community as expressed through the ballot box. This is not to argue that governments are always powerful enough to achieve their policy objectives but, rather, that governments are free to utilize the material, social, economic and political assets of the community to promote common interests in accordance with the principles of democracy. The autonomy of a democratic state is assumed not to be constrained by external factors beyond those that arise from its relative power position within the international order.

The final assumption is that the democratic state acts in the interests of the whole of the people, not in the interests of particular national or global interests. There is an obvious tension between the liberal and democratic elements of liberal democracy, which is often expressed in terms of the limits to individual freedom and rights and the distinction liberals often make between the public and private spheres, political and economic life and the roles of the state and civil society (Beetham 1992). The social demand for greater freedom in the private sphere contrasts with the need to pursue the common good, often through policies that make provision for excluded groups, if not in the name of social justice then in the name of social order (Held 1992). The democratic state is therefore a limited state, a state that attempts to reconcile individual freedom exercised in the pursuit of wealth with state intervention exercised as a necessary condition for social order.

The dominant assumptions surrounding ideas of democracy, including the state as the appropriate community, accountability, autonomy and the national interest, have meant that little attention had been given to understanding new forms of democracy more appropriate in the age of globalization. As David Held has pointed out:

> ... the very idea of consent through elections, and the particular notion that relevant constituencies of voluntary agreement are the communities of bounded territory or a state, becomes problematic as soon as the issue of national, regional and global interconnectedness is considered and the nature of a so-called 'relevant community' is contested. Whose consent is necessary and whose participation is justified in decisions concerning, for instance, AIDS, or acid rain, or the use of nonrenewable resources? (Held 1992: 22)

We might add universal human rights, including economic, social, civil and political rights, to Held's brief list of global issues that draw into question the generally held assumptions of democracy. For Held, the most striking feature of the global demand for democracy, in its most widely acknowledged form, is that it is emerging 'just at that moment when the very efficacy of democracy as a national form of political organization appears open to question' (Held 1992: 31).

Several features of globalization challenge the current understanding of national democracy. First, the assumption that governments remain in control of state borders cannot be sustained under conditions of globalization, where economic flows, ideas, cultural exchanges, social interactions and political interconnectedness are widening and deepening (Held & McGrew 1993, 1999). The development of new technology enables the formation of new transnational relationships that challenge the territorial limits of democracy, raising the question of how to define the appropriate democratic community. If some groups possess the capabilities to free themselves from the regulatory machinery of governments by using technology, then the globalization of economic, social and political relations places them beyond the democratically constituted controls of the state.

Second, globalization has seen state power decline as transnational processes grow in scale and number. This is evident in the growing intensity of global economic, social and political interconnectedness that threatens the capacity of the state in its role as the guardian of the 'common good' and the national interest. The power of TNCs, with annual budgets greater than that of many states, is the most visible sign of this change (see Chapter 3). Instead of acting in the interests of the community as a whole, in important areas of social, economic and political life the role of the state is reduced to that of an administrator, to oversee and enforce regulations that emerge from decisions made at the global level, for example, global trade regulations (Evans 1999). Consequently, decisions that are beyond the reach of democratically elected governments constrain the capacity of the sovereign democratic state in important economic, political, social and legal aspects of citizens' lives.

A third feature of globalization that challenges the dominant understanding of democracy follows from the above. As economic and political life becomes more complex, many traditional functions of the state are transferred to global and regional international organizations. States therefore surrender their sovereignty to larger political units such as the European Union, the North Atlantic Treaty Organization (NATO), the World Bank and the World Trade Organization (WTO). As critics have observed, the WTO already has the authority to 'strike down particular national interests, even when these are enshrined in law or custom', creating a model for a future world order in which the state plays a lesser role (George 1999: 22). Given the growing authority of these organizations, the assumption that national democratic communities 'make and determine decision and policies for themselves' or that governments 'determine what is right or appropriate exclusively for their own citizens' seems doubtful (Held 1992: 21). As the former secretary-general of the Commonwealth, Shridath Ramphal has noted, many of these organizations are looking and acting like 'self-appointed presidium', a recent phenomenon that has escaped the attention of most political leaders and commentators. However, 'the democracy idea has a larger reach than national frontiers. Democracy at the national level but authoritarianism in the global homeland – these are contradictions in terms' (Ramphal 1992).

The conclusion drawn by Held and other commentators from this analysis is that the state is losing its autonomy because of decisions made from above, at the global level, raising questions that challenge the generally held assumptions about democratic representation and the accountability of government. The response from below, at the local level, is to challenge the authority and legitimacy of the existing institutions of democracy, which are perceived as no longer capable of promoting the interests of citizens or protecting their human rights satisfactorily. While the formal rights represented by a democratic constitution may offer some assurance that the state has an obligation to protect the human rights of its citizens, the policies, actions, decisions and authority of transnational organizations and corporations weaken the state's ability to deliver on those rights. Similarly, although international law presents the state as the main guarantor of human rights, the state may not possess the capabilities to fulfil its obligations. Instead of creating a post-Cold War order that offers the prospects for protecting human rights through democracy and the rule of law, globalization has created the conditions for disorder, authoritarian rule beyond the territorial state, the reformation of the state entity and the potential for continued violations of human rights (McCorquodale & Fairbrother 1999: 758). For those who continue to put their faith in democracy, the assertion that the 'great beauty of globalization is that no one is in control' (Hormats 1998), offers a chilling reminder that democracy at the state level will not be enough.

If these conclusions are apposite, then the assumed close relationship between democracy and human rights may not be as secure as the dominant version of democracy anticipates. If the democratic state is no longer fully accountable to the people, if the state is losing its autonomy, and if the interests of the whole of the people are no longer served by national systems of democracy, then the 'universal acclaim that democracy enjoys at this historic moment does not mean that all is well with democracy' (Johansen 1993: 213). What this means for universal human rights is the subject of the remainder of this chapter.

Democracy and Universal Human Rights

A recent example of the confusion over democracy and human rights is seen in the Human Rights Watch report on Latin America and the Caribbean. At the onset, the report asserts that 'multiparty democracies appear stable throughout most of Latin America and the Caribbean' (HRW 1999: 1). However, the body of the report is concerned with detailing the failure of many states in the region either to protect human rights or to fulfil their responsibilities under international law. More tellingly, the report details recent measures to withdraw from human rights obligations previously accepted. For example, the government of Trinidad and Tobago announced in May 1998 that it was considering withdrawing from the American Convention on Human Rights and the First Protocol of the International Covenant on Civil and Political Rights (ICCPR). This follows the withdrawal of Jamaica from the First Optional Protocol of the ICCPR in 1997, allegedly in an attempt to avoid further scrutiny of its current policy on capital punishment. The report also notes the attitude of several Latin American leaders, including President Alvaro Arzú of Guatemala who has denounced organizations like Human Rights Watch as 'sly instruments of foreign policy', self-appointed spokespeople 'whose representativeness is debatable'. In a similar vein, President Carlos Menem claims that Argentina is willing to sacrifice human rights protection in the service of fighting crime, which Menem argues can only be achieved by overlooking the extra-legal actions of the police (HRW 1999: 6). Similar examples of human rights abuses in democratic states are not difficult to find, for example, the Narmada Dam project in India, the treatment of the Ogoni people in Nigeria and military brutality in Chiapas, Mexico (Adeola 2000; Flinchum 1998).

It is clear from these examples that we must treat the claim that human rights and democracy share a symbiotic relationship with great caution. For many students of democracy, this will come as no surprise. While all theories of democracy include a concern for rights, historically such rights were never extended to all people sharing a common territory. Athenian democracy, for example, bestowed rights only on adult males born in Athens, an exclusionary practice that denied formal political participation to women and slaves. Some have even argued that the denial of rights to women and slaves provided the mechanism through which male citizens acquired the necessary time to participate in democracy (Arat 1991). It follows from this that if a commitment to democracy does not necessarily mean a commitment to equal rights, it cannot imply a commitment to universal human rights. Indeed, any attempt to legitimate a set of universal human rights represents a threat to a democratic community's claim to autonomy, self-determination and the right to decide upon its own particular political, economic and social order.

Yet even if we accept that national democracy by itself could deliver human rights, it is doubtful whether this could be sustained under conditions of globalization. Although some authors have argued that growing economic interdependence brings a parallel growth in 'moral interdependence', global society shows few signs of democratizing itself as a solution to the potential failure of national governments to protect human rights (Donnelly 1986: 618). One consequence of globalization is that it is no longer possible – if it ever was – to understand development, security, environmental degradation or human rights as exclusively national problems. And if they are not exclusively national problems then the institutions of national democracy alone cannot be expected to provide a framework for people to participate in seeking solutions. Furthermore, under conditions of globalization, governments seem increasingly unable to exercise the necessary authority to secure democratic outcomes or offer protection for human rights, particularly economic and social rights (Gill 1996). Therefore, if we are serious about protecting human rights, it will not be enough to enhance the institutions and practices of liberal democracy at the national level alone. While strengthening national institutions must support democracy, ensuring that deprived, marginalized and forgotten groups can exercise their right to participation, this will achieve little unless global society itself is democratized (Sakamoto 1991).

In this respect, the United Nations is often thought of as the first step in democratizing global politics. The UN's role in the field of human rights is, however, paradoxical. On the one hand, the impressive body of international law on human rights generated by the UN has stimulated extensive debate in a wide range of national and international forums. This has kept the 'idea' of human rights at the centre of global politics and engaged the interest of a growing number of non-governmental organizations (NGOs) devoted to securing justice and the protection of human rights throughout the world. It has also prompted a shift in the international normative order, if only because the addition of human rights to the international political agenda 'alters the day-to-day conduct of international relations', with human rights demanding more attention, and of a different kind, than in the past (Ruggie 1983: 100). In this way, the United Nations has contributed to the global reach of the 'idea' of universal human rights. On the other hand, as an organization based upon sovereign equality and non-intervention, the UN cannot respond to the demand for universal human rights it has itself engendered. This is reflected in the claim that the UN is good at setting standards, but poor at implementing those standards. In short, the UN remains responsive to the demands of states, not to people and their demand for rights (Felice 1999).

Democracy and Global Order

Why then have the generally held assumptions about human rights and democracy been so vigorously promoted in some quarters? The answer to this question is found by looking at the failure of development in the less developed world. According to this argument, the threat of social unrest, which would disrupt the supply of raw materials, restrict investment opportunities and severely damage prospects for exploiting low-cost labour, cannot be avoided by using coercive policing and military suppression, as it was during the Cold War period. During the Cold War such coercion was legitimated by the argument that the threat of communism justified support for any tyrannical government provided it was avowedly anti-communist (Mahbubani 1992). Violence was justified 'because the Third World people were being killed to protect them from the evil incarnate – communism' (Shivji 1999: 257). The collapse of the Soviet bloc removed this rationale for maintaining order at the expense of human rights and justice. Instead, policy makers turned to democracy as the moral justification for maintaining economic and political relations with governments known to violate human rights.

This left those who trade with repressive regimes, or those who want to maintain cordial relations for political reasons, with the dilemma of promoting a new rationale that justified continuing economic and political relations. The distinction between author-itarian and totalitarian regimes, which assumes that the former represents a transitory stage in the move to full democracy, while the latter does not, offers a well-known foundation for resolving this dilemma (Kirkpatrick 1982). The success of this move can be judged by the way that the democracy discourse increasingly replaces the human rights discourse in US foreign policy circles (Carothers 1994). Through this device, it remains legitimate to continue with economic relationships, to call for extended aid programmes and to develop new trade and business relations, unhindered by moral concerns, provided a country has created the institutions of democracy.

However, the promotion of democracy was not necessarily concerned with social justice, human rights, human security or ideas of human worth, but the need to create an appropriate global order for the continued expansion of global capital. In support of this aim, powerful capitalist states sought to promote democracy in its procedural guise: as a set of democratic institutions rather than as a means of achieving social and economic transformation that would have empowered the poor and the socially excluded. This form of 'low-intensity democracy' may be understood as a component of 'low-intensity conflict', a policy that the US sought to promote as a means of securing anti-communist and anti-reformist support that avoided either unstable representative democratic systems or military dictatorship:

Democracy was thus used as a form of intervention. Its intent was to pre-empt either progressive reform or revolutionary change. Beyond seeking to demobilise popular forces, it also sought to legitimise the *status quo*. Authoritarianism was thus discredited and delegitimised. The new 'democratic' regime, which temporarily enjoys increased legitimacy, can in fact undertake economic and social policies of 'adjustment' that impose new hardships on the general population and compromise economic sovereignty. The paradox of Low Intensity Democracy is that a civilianised conservative regime can pursue painful and even repressive social and economic policies with more impunity and with less popular resistance than can an openly authoritarian regime. From the point of view of the US and conservative domestic elites in these countries, this quality must make it an interesting and useful alternative to traditional overt authoritarianism. (Gills, Rocamora & Wilson 1993: 8)

This paradox does not escape the consciousness of citizens where low-intensity democracy operates. As incidents of resistance to globalization often remind us, the economic conditions suffered by many people, together with an absence of basic liberties, stimulates challenges to established systems of government, which are seen 'domestically as predatory and corrupt and internationally, servile executors of the economic agenda of ruling classes of the major OECD nations' (Cheru 1997: 164).

By adopting a definition of democracy that places emphasis on the creation of formal institutions, which promises limited changes to civil and political rights but has little to say about economic and social reform, 'repressive abuses of human rights continue usually against the familiar targets of labour, students, the left and human rights activists' (Gills, Rocamora & Wilson 1993: 21). For those countries who adopt the institutions of low-intensity democracy, the economic support offered by international financial institutions and aid programmes, together with the promise of corporate investment, is conditional upon maintaining a particular type of democracy that plays a crucial role in maintaining the conditions of globalization. If reformist groups attempt to transcend the limitations imposed by low-intensity democracy, and instead promote a version of popular democracy that includes social reform and justice, then support is withdrawn and the spectre of military intervention surfaces (Chomsky 1998). In short, democracy often means little more than a 'thin veneer of Western concepts', including national sovereignty, statehood, parliamentary institutions and the 'rule of law', all of which are intended to subdue ethnic, cultural and religious tensions in the effort to secure an order fit for economic growth and development (Mahbubani 1992).

For critics of democracy, however, the claim to have established a democratic form of government must rest upon something more than the introduction of formal institutions, which often do nothing to provide for social, economic and political reforms or the rights of the people. In countries where low-intensity democracy operates, governments give little attention to developing an open, rights-based culture. On the contrary, the governments of low-intensity democracies commonly work to ensure that trade unions are weak, wages are kept at a level beneath that necessary for a dignified life, non-governmental organizations are marginalized or declared illegal and the press and media are censored. The practice of offering fledgling democracies technical and training assistance to strengthen some state institutions – the police and the military, for example – can provide the means for maintaining a domestic order that pays little attention to human rights and social justice (Carothers 1994; HRW 1999). Furthermore, the social structures and traditions that support low-intensity democracy often mean that in practice access to public office is restricted to particular groups. While the existence of the institutions of democracy may help to legitimate external relations, particularly where the established democracies of advanced technological states remain squeamish about trading with authoritarian governments, the protection of universal human rights is not necessarily guaranteed. Although some commentators defend the introduction of low-intensity democracy, arguing that it is the first stage in a journey that ends in full democratic participation and social reform, Gills, Rocamora and Wilson argue that it is more accurate to understanding it as an end in itself – as a way of maintaining an order that supports the interests of global and national capital.

These arguments are refuted by some authors who suggest that a right to democracy is also a human right, not only under international law but increasingly as an actual right observable in the practice of states (Frank 1988). Frank argues that this right to a democratic form of government is built upon the right to self-determination, which replaced the previously accepted norm of colonialism at the end of the Second World War (Art. 1 of the UN Charter). According to Frank, this claim is further supported by the norm of self-determination, established under Article 21 of the Universal Declaration of Human Rights, which gives everyone 'the right to take part in the government of his [sic] country ... expressed in periodic and genuine elections which shall be by universal suffrage and shall be held by secret vote or by equivalent free voting processes'. Article 1 of both the ICCPR and the International Covenant on Economic, Social and Cultural Rights (ICESCR), which asserts that 'All peoples have the right of self-determination', lends further support to Frank's claim. Similarly, the regional human rights regimes of Europe and Africa acknowledge the right to self-determination and democratic representation.

Frank's argument, however, remains embedded in the idea of national democracy. In Frank's view, the territorial state continues to define the limits of the democratic community. All that is necessary to satisfy the human right to democratic government is the creation and maintenance of national democratic institutions, including periodic elections and a representative assembly. Frank has little to say about the need to democratize the global institutions of global governance, the impact of globalization on the realization of democracy or the human rights consequences of the form of democracy he seeks to promote. To repeat, under conditions of globalization, limiting the scope of our thinking to the national democratic community may not be enough. If the decision and actions of transnational actors are not democratically accountable, but none the less have consequences for the life chances, human security and human rights of individuals and communities (Cox 1997), democracy practised at the national level may have limited value. Furthermore, it remains unclear how a right to democracy necessarily follows from a right to self-determination, since self-determination must permit a people to decide its own political system and form of government.

In cases where the creation of low-intensity democracy fails to silence dissent, governments seek new strategies for coping with social unrest. Robert Cox has suggested that these new strategies can be divided into two broad categories: 'poor relief' and 'riot control'. Cox argues that the growing number and importance of non-governmental organizations devoted to humanitarian aid, which parallels the importance that the United Nations attaches to humanitarian assistance, offers the most tangible evidence of the poor relief element. When both low-intensity democracy and poor relief fail to prevent political and economic destabilization, governments resort to employing military force. Thus, poor relief and riot control 'help to sustain the emerging social structure of the world by minimizing the risk of chaos in the bottom layer' (Cox 1997: 58). In this view, democracy and human rights are of limited interest when social unrest threatens the smooth continuation of the practices of globalization. Decision makers rarely ask questions about accountability when the maintenance of the global political economy is at stake.

This raises questions to do with the potential for the democratization of world order, including the protection of human rights. On the one hand, some authors suggest that liberal democracy and a good human rights record are increasingly necessary if a state is to achieve and maintain global legitimacy (Hoffman 1988). The future for liberal democracy and human rights therefore seems bright, because globalization means that no state can escape detailed public scrutiny. The work of NGOs and their use of communications technology is significant in this respect. On the other hand, if the state has less political and economic significance under conditions of globalization, state legitimacy may not be of great importance. To achieve democracy and human rights under conditions of globalization therefore requires us to abandon traditional thinking on the state and world order. Instead, globalization theory urges us to take a more inclusive view of the global political economy, including our understanding of democracy, with a view to creating new expressions of global democratic governance. Frank's optimistic view – that a right to democracy is already accepted under international law – may therefore offer unintended support to those whose interests are best served by maintaining the centrality of the state system when thinking about the democratization of world order.

Development, Democracy and Human Rights

The above discussion has attempted to point to the dangers of substituting the language of democracy for that of human rights. More particularly, it has attempted to demonstrate that the effort to promote the dominant version of democracy has more to do with maintaining an order that serves the interests of global capital, rather than the interests of those whose human rights and security are constantly threatened. Fostering the assumption that '*by definition* promoting democracy entails promoting human rights', provides a rationale for foreign policy interventions intended to secure a form of government sympathetic to the aims of the neoliberal consensus (Carothers 1994: 109, original emphasis). Frank's attempt to argue that democracy is itself a human right lends support to this argument. Should a state fail to provide the conditions necessary for promoting the values associated with the neoliberal consensus, it is then possible to argue that intervention is justified, not on the grounds of economic interests but, more nobly, in the cause of populations deprived of the right to democracy. Moreover, the widely accepted configuration of democracy, the free market and human rights, which reflects the values of the neoliberal consensus, further justifies the use or threat of force against those who attempt to voice an alternative view.

This section looks at some of the issues surrounding development, democracy and human rights that follow from the above discussion. Although all states pursue economic development and growth, in the current period of globalization it might be argued that these goals are 'profoundly anti-democratic' for two sets of reasons: one concerned with the domestic context of democracy and the other with the global context (McCorquodale & Fairbrother 1999).

Within the domestic context, the right to development is defined as the right of 'every human person and all peoples to participate in, contribute to, and enjoy economic, social, cultural and political development, in which all human rights and fundamental freedoms can be fully realized' (Declaration on the Right to Development 1986, Art. 1). However, the dominant understanding of development tends to ignore all but the goal of economic development at the expense of social, cultural and political development. Following arguments encountered in earlier chapters – that globalization provides the conditions for privileging economic development over social welfare and human rights (Clark 1999, Ch. 6) – some scholars argue that the policy of sacrificing the rights of some for the good of others or future generations is the accepted wisdom of elites in all countries, not merely developing countries (Tomasevski 1989). The most visible evidence for this conclusion is seen in the practice of assessing development by reference to economic growth rates, gross domestic product (GDP) and the success of efficiency-maximizing strategies. Although the Human Development Index, published annually by the United Nations Development Programme (UNDP) in its *Human Development Report*, attempts to reverse this trend, the economic element of development continues to dominate the thinking and language of most leaders. Following this limited definition, development becomes an end in itself, rather than a means to an end, which would offer an alternative definition that placed human rights, democracy and social justice at its centre (Sieghart 1983). Making this observation, critics argue that it is not possible to 'talk your way to democracy in the language of development economics [because] liberty and justice do not exist as technical terms in economic science' (Lummis 1991: 52).

A second assumption that informs the politics of the domestic context is that full economic development is a realistic goal for all. This assumption is predicated upon the premise that levels of consumption, such as those achieved in the US and other Western economies, is a viable goal for all people. Following from this is the further assumption that a fully developed world will see current inequalities gradually narrowed and finally abolished. However, according to the 1998 United Nations *Human Development Report*, the top 20% of the world's highest income counties account for 86% of total private consumption, while the poorest 20% account for a mere 1.3%. Furthermore, the richest 20% consume 45% of all meat and fish, compared to the poorest 20% who consume 5%, and 58% of total energy, compared to 4% by the poorest 20%. The report also notes that these cross-country comparisons conceal continuing high levels of poverty and deprivation in all industrialized countries, with an estimated 100 million people in developed countries suffering deprivation similar to those in less developed countries (UNDP 1998). Given these statistics, it is difficult to see just how the promotion of democracy can be achieved through a model of development that is demonstrably failing to achieve a reduction in inequalities. Perhaps more tellingly, the UNDP notes that although consumption has doubled in the US compared to the 1950s, the percentage of Americans calling themselves 'happy' has declined steadily since 1957 (UNDP 1998).

If popular movements do raise the issue of democratic participation when investment banks, aid donors and corporations engage in development programmes, the focus is rarely on questions about whether the people support national policy objectives that lead to rapid changes in social life, social dislocation and loss of livelihood. Instead, project managers take the objective of rapid economic growth and development as a given. Popular resistance is then understood as a failure to consult with national and local groups at the planning stage, following the decision to proceed with a project. Participation is appropriate if it helps the smooth running of a project by deflecting unwanted public attention and defusing the potential for social unrest. As UNDP-sponsored research has noted, however, the failure to appreciate the distinction between resistance associated with a rejection of the 'common sense' of rapid economic growth and development as a policy objective and the rejection of a particular project, offers an insight into why programmes sponsored by the World Bank continue to attract antagonism (Taylor & Pieper, undated). World Bank officials have argued, for example, that care should be taken to invest in the social infrastructure of a community, particularly where 'resettlement' is an issue, before projects begin, to avoid delays caused by social protest and resistance. The Bank's anxiety to gain post-decision legitimation is further seen when the 'problem of identifying *appropriate* community-based organizations for the project's participatory component' (Bhatnager 1992: 17, emphasis added). Since there are often difficulties in getting agreement between donors, borrowing governments, Bank officials and local people on what participation means, and who should have a legitimate right to participate, the selection of *appropriate* participants becomes a vital issue that 'serves merely as a way to get people to agree with what the project wants to do' (Dichter 1992: 92).

A final reason why development might be seen as anti-democratic also concerns the 'common-sense' model of development, because it draws attention away from political goals, including the demand for human rights, and instead places the focus on economic goals. As economic development is understood increasingly as the central aim of all governments, the deprivations suffered by those whose environment is degraded, culture devastated, freedom to protest peacefully suppressed and traditional ties with the land forcibly severed are seen less as the victims of human rights violations and more as the unfortunate citizens who must bear the cost of economic progress for the good of the wider community (Tomasevski 1989; Kotheri 1994). Those who continue to protest are referred to pejoratively as insular, conservative and traditionalist, bent on denying the benefits of modernization to the mass of the people.

The strategy adopted by some states in response to both the demands of globalization from above and the demand for democracy from below – referred to by one commentator as 'authoritarian democracy' (Mittelman 1995) – attempts to take advantage of globalization while offering its citizens a measure of participation, although not at the expense of a failure to achieve economic growth and development. Although 'in theory democracy means accountability to the governed, in practice leaders are accountable to market forces, most notably debt structures and structural adjustment programs' (Mittelman 1996: 9). This attitude reinforces the view that government is about achieving economic progress rather than good governance, democracy, human security and human rights. While these goals may be desirable, the global neoliberal consensus argues that achieving these values must follow success in economic growth and development, not precede it.

The emphasis on economic development that is central to both the discourse on universal human rights and the discourse on democracy has given many governments an opportunity to plead for special tolerance of their human rights record. This argument was encountered earlier in Chapter 1, during the discussion on globalization. Many of these governments argue that their attitude to human rights is conditioned by two important factors that do not pertain in developing countries. The first is the need to build a nation on the remains of colonial institutions. These governments argue that their priority is stability: when thinking about human rights, does the promotion of a particular human right help or hinder the process of nation building and the move from a postcolonial to a mature state? Second, these governments embrace the idea that economic development is of paramount importance to the long-term stability and security of the nation. Governments must not allow traditional values and alternative versions of development to deflect the nation from achieving the goal of economic development. Suppression and coercion of those who attempt to stand in the way of necessary social, cultural and political change is therefore legitimate, in the interests of future generations (Tamilmoran 1992).

Furthermore, many leaders in less developed countries argue that the history of the West demonstrates that human rights and democracy came onto the agenda following the effort to achieve economic development. The leaders of less developed countries therefore accuse developed states of placing the 'democratic cart' before the 'economic horse' (Mahbubani 1992). Moreover, these leaders often point to the deep tribal, ethnic, family and religious divisions within their countries, which they argue cannot be overcome simply by transplanting forms of democracy established in developed countries over many centuries. Accordingly, national leaders argue that social divisions offer a hostile context in which to develop the institutions of democracy because they represent a barrier to developing a politically active middle class, which most accounts see as a prerequisite for democracy (Kotheri 1994). Additionally, leaders in developing countries are prone to reminding the developed world of the historic consequences of imperialism, which, they argue, was instrumental in impoverishing current populations. For these reasons, nation building becomes a code for the strong state, which is a prerequisite for stability, foreign investment and the guarantee of a 'cheap, docile and disciplined labour force' (Mandani et al. 1993). Before tackling issues of democracy and human rights, governments must achieve the transition from less developed to developed status successfully.

Therefore, leaders in developing states argue that their first task is to build a strong economy that nurtures the common interests of the middle classes, breaks down traditional ties and provides the economic conditions for democracy and human rights. Typical of this approach is that of Kishore Mahbubani, who argues that conditions in most developing states necessitate a 'period of strong and firm government', committed to radical social reform in order to 'break out of the vicious circle of poverty sustained by social structures contained in vested interests opposed to real change' (Mahbubani 1992: 8). Those who support this approach point to the success of authoritarian governments who achieved the so-called East Asian 'miracle', where governments promoted a very circumscribed definition of both democracy and human rights. The collapse of these economies during late 1997 and early 1998 only serves to remind political leaders and economic interests that the demand for democracy and human rights may bring economic collapse, which must be countered by strengthening 'market-preserving authoritarianism' (Davis 1998: 312).

These sentiments were forcefully articulated by Asian leaders during the 1993 Vienna Conference on Human Rights. Stressing the particularity of Asian society, Asian leaders sought to present an approach to human rights, based upon 'Asian values', that distinguished it from the dominant Western approach. Important among these Asian values are respect for authority, deference to societal interests, emphasis on duty, the politics of consensus rather than conflict and the centrality of the family in all social relations (Mahbubani 1992; Mauzy 1997; Freeman 1995, 1996). According to Asian leaders, the West's approach to human rights, which stresses the importance of freedom as an end in itself, leads to a 'vulgar individualism' that separates rights from responsibilities and duties (Muzaffar 1995). In contrast to the West, Asian society understands individual freedom as a means to an end that seeks to promote the collective interest of the whole of the community. According to many Asian leaders, the West should recognize that the social and economic costs of illegal drugs, divorce, family breakdown, single-parent families and rising crime rates owe much to the cult of individualism, which the Asian tradition does not recognize (Woodiwiss 1998).

From the perspective of many East Asian countries, the immediate task is to build upon the economic success achieved during the last two decades, by developing a sense of national identity, clearly differentiated from that identity associated with their colonial past (Tang 1995). Part of the process of achieving this aim is to assert Asian values in the field of human rights, since the conception of universal human rights developed through the United Nations regime takes no account of any Asian tradition, for example, Confucianism or Buddhism. Through asserting a conception of universal human rights based upon Asian values, Asian countries seek to reflect their new and elevated status within the global political economy and to free themselves from the last vestiges of colonial influence and control. Fortuitously, Asian values also support policies that protect markets by legitimating state non-intervention, most importantly, in areas of economic life that promote the conditions necessary to attract investment, for example, wage controls, environmental protection and levels of social expenditure. Consequently, economic interests based in non-Asian economies argue that the attempt to promote Asian values, as an alternative to universally recognized human rights, is more concerned with attracting investment and securing a competitive advantage by offering a disciplined workforce and less burdensome restrictions on corporate behaviour (Tang 1995). Thus, as one scholar has observed, while 'the doctrine of human rights can be misused to disguise Western neo-imperialism, the doctrine of cultural relativism can be misused to conceal or justify oppression by Asian states' (Freeman 1995: 15).

Furthermore, promoting Asian values as an alternative vision of human rights offers an opportunity to reject any attempt to implement universal standards through the use of conditionality. According to Asian countries, human rights conditionality reinforces several attitudes that are no longer appropriate in the current global political economy. Among these is the old imperial ethos that 'right is might', the assumption that human rights violations occur only in less developed countries and that it is rational to promote civil and political rights by denying access to aid intended to promote economic and social rights (Mauzy 1997; Boyle 1995). In short, by emphasizing the moral, social and cultural differences between Asian and Western countries, Asian leaders seek to promote an alternative vision of human rights that supports Asian economic interests and provides a defence against external criticism of current human rights practices (Caballero-Anthony 1995).

Finally, at the domestic level, the political culture of many less developed countries makes little distinction between wealth and politics, making it less possible to separate capitalist accumulation from political control (Taylor & Pieper, undated). Globalization enables wider access to media images that allow the masses to compare their own standards of living with those enjoyed by both the West and the wealthy in their own societies. This often leads to a growing sense of inequality and, consequently, to social and political pressure for policies that promise higher incomes and access to goods currently enjoyed only by the few. Should leaders fail to respond to these demands, particularly when the introduction of 'low-intensity democracy' promises greater accountability, increasing social tensions may lead to social disruption, threatening the authority of social groups accustomed to assuming the reins of power. This often leads to coercive measures intended to suppress the demand for greater equality, which threatens the goal of ever greater economic development. Despite the fact that governments organize such coercive action, it is worth noting that such action is encouraged and supported by the military aid, technology transfers and financial incentives offered by those with an interest in supporting a low-wage, docile workforce (Arat 1991).

If the domestic context suggests that the creation and maintenance of the institutions of democracy do not necessarily deliver a culture of rights, the global context is no more encouraging. The move to introduce both financial and trade liberalization on a global scale, managed by organizations like the WTO and the World Bank, further weakens the potential for people to exercise any claim for democratic governance. An examination of levels of participation, representation and accountability demonstrates the paucity of democracy at the global level.

The argument that the majority are excluded from participating in the current drive to liberalize global markets focuses on the activities of the WTO, which is often seen as the embryo for a global governing authority (George 1999). According to critics, participation in developing the substance of WTO rules and decision-making procedures often means that greater attention is given to the interests of transnational capital rather than to rights and human security. Martin Khor of the Third World Network, argues that rule- and decision-making processes at the WTO display an 'utter disrespect for democratic participation of the majority of Members [of the WTO]'. This is manifest in the practice of convening small groups, with memberships that include only the advanced capitalist states, to discuss and develop the WTO position on particular issues. It is also seen in the lack of transparency during negotiations and the non-incorporation of views expressed by less developed countries in the working drafts of proposed trade agreements (Khor 2000). The outcome of these tactics is that many trade agreements and declarations reflect a harmony of interests within the developed world, rather than a 'consensus' resulting from negotiations that allow the full participation of all countries. As Khor argues:

> The process of decision-making and negotiations in the WTO has to be democratised and made transparent. 'Green Room' meetings should be discontinued. Every Member, however small, must have the right to know what negotiations are taking place, and to take part in them. Until the reforms to the system and to the substance of the WTO take place, the organisation's credibility will remain low. (Khor 2000)

Similarly, the activities of the World Bank often make it impossible for people to exercise a right to democratic representation because they are not allowed to participate in the decision-making processes associated with economic development. The Bank often supports projects aimed at certain types of development that do not necessarily benefit the majority. Many of these are large-scale projects that directly lead to human rights violations by displacing people, destroying their environment and denying access to traditional lands used for agriculture or hunting. When those who suffer these violations of economic, social and cultural rights attempt to organize resistance to such development, civil and political rights are frequently denied (see Chapter 3). This is hardly surprising, since the World Bank, in common with other international financial institutions, is more concerned with creating the necessary conditions for the smooth running of the global free market, not in assisting in delivering human rights. The Bank's concerns are external to the needs of the people and cannot focus on education, welfare, jobs, subsistence and the other factors of human security (McCorquodale & Fairbrother 1999). In other words, a clear distinction must always be drawn between human rights and economic interests.

For critics of WTO and World Bank practices, liberalization is 'imposed' upon people who are excluded from full participation in the decision-making processes that directly affect their ability to claim human rights. Those who plead for 'special and different treatment', including the time to implement changes to avoid the worst social consequences of new liberalization regulations, are rarely listened to (Chimni 1999: 341–2). Even when less powerful groups are offered a role in these processes, a lack of resources severely limits their ability to follow the detail of negotiations, and to understand the full implications of agreements. Although liberalization often leads to a denial of economic and social rights, a decline in the ability of the state to act autonomously in the interests of its people and a denial of democratic participation, developed economies continue to press for further deregulation. As Susan George has noted, consumerism is the only form of participation widely acknowledged by proponents of liberalization. The 'superfluous billions' unable to engage in the liberal, free market, consumer-oriented global order do not qualify for a voice in shaping a future global order (George 1999).

Representation at the formal discussions on further liberalization is also deficient. Formally, all members of the WTO enjoy equal status within the organization. However, many less developed countries do not possess the resources to support a permanent representative at WTO headquarters in Geneva. Recent research by Christian Aid shows that over half of the less developed countries have no representation in Geneva:

> These countries have a total population of 81 million people who, despite being members, have no voice at all at the WTO. Those developing countries that do have some representation in Geneva often have only one person responsible for all negotiations in the WTO, where there can be more than 40 meetings a week on subjects ranging from air transport to competition

policy, environmental agreements to industrial tariffs. By contrast the US has over 250 negotiators at Geneva, and richer countries frequently fly in technical experts to deal with complex issues. (Christian Aid, 1999)

In the absence of any system that supports the capacity of poor countries to participate in all the important discussions at the WTO, developing countries cannot hope to 'follow the negotiations, let alone participate actively [or] understand what they are committing themselves to' (Khor 2000).

It is also doubtful if even those countries with the resources to fund a permanent delegation in Geneva represent the best interest of their citizens on human security and human rights. The close relationship between WTO delegations and the representatives of global business and finance suggests that the interests of the poor are of little concern. Again, Christian Aid notes that Cargill, a company that controls half the global trade in grains, 'was heavily involved in preparations for the US negotiating position on agriculture before the last round of trade talks – with some commentators claiming that the company wrote the first draft of the US negotiating position' (Christian Aid 1999). Similarly, business groups were extensively canvassed by the European Union during the process of drafting a proposal for an investment agreement, although other interest groups were excluded. In a further case, the Australian delegation included eight representatives of business but rejected all attempts by NGOs and trade unions to gain a seat (Christian Aid 1999). In effect, this means that the interests of the majority of the world's peoples are denied a voice in important negotiations and decision-making processes that help shape their lives.

The message that this transmits across the globe is that satisfying the interests of transnational capital, by providing the conditions for an efficient global economy, is the primary objective of liberalization: all other values, including universal human rights, must be sacrificed to this cause. At the centre of this project is what Susan George has recently referred to as the 'fast caste', or those who have access to knowledge and the formal structures for decision making. Members of the fast caste have no loyalty to any particular country, nation or community beyond their own business associates, whose interests they attempt to represent and promote (George 1999). To give some scale to this assertion, the UNDP estimates that of the forty thousand TNCs currently operating in the global economy, the top one hundred control one-fifth of all TNC assets. Furthermore, one-third of all world trade is now intra-firm and a further third is inter-firm. In those cases where NGOs are allowed access to negotiations on liberalization,

WTO officials and delegation members often receive them with a courteousness that is often mistaken for influence (Taylor 1998). Reinforcing Taylor's observation, George argues that assuming that any change:

> ... because it would contribute to justice, equity and peace, need only be explained to be adopted is the saddest and most irritating kind of naivety. Many good, otherwise intelligent people seem to believe that once powerful individuals and institutions have actually *understood* the gravity of the crisis (any crisis) and the urgent need for its remedy, they will smack their brow, admit they have been wrong all along and, in a fit of revelation, instantly redirect their behaviour by 180 degrees. (George 1999: 181, original emphasis)

Finally, as some commentators have pointed out (Khor 2000; Coote 1996), the decision-making procedures of the WTO are often secretive, protecting decision makers from all attempts to make them accountable. The practice of 'Green Room meetings', which are not officially announced, not mandated by the full membership of the WTO and rarely publish their conclusions, has already been mentioned above. The WTO dispute settlement mechanism established under the Final Act of the Uruguay Round, gave considerable powers to ensure compliance with trade rules, no matter the labour, environmental, social and human rights consequences for some people. However, a dispute settlement panel 'meets without observers and their documents, transcripts and proceedings are not disclosed' (George 1999: 22). Furthermore, although the dispute settlement procedures do make provision for appeals, this hardly measures up to the levels of accountability expected when decisions might damage the social and human rights prospects of millions of people. Lacking transparency, developing countries often treat dispute settlement with suspicion and accuse the developed economies of using the WTO to enforce market discipline on the weak while denying access to their own markets.

Conclusion

This chapter has attempted to argue that human rights and democracy do not necessarily share a symbiotic relationship, as is often assumed. Although the imagery of democracy has achieved a high profile in global and international politics in recent years, the discussion here points to a political rationale that has little to do with achieving the conditions for protecting and promoting human rights. Instead, the image of democracy is used to legitimate forms of behaviour supportive of particular economic interests associated with globalization. Held and Hindess, for example, argue that national forms of democracy are incapable of providing a culture of rights until we recognize the need to democratize both the institutions that operate *above* the state, at the global level and those *below* the state, at the local level (Held 1991, 1992 & 1995; Hindess 1991, 1992 & 1999). Gill, Rocamora and Wilson also recognize this need in their conceptualization of 'low-intensity democracy' (Gills, Rocamora & Wilson 1993), which is more concerned with the formal creation of institutions than with democratic outcome.

At the national level, the idea of a democratically elected government, representing the interests of a bounded community, seems less possible, given the context of globalization and a widely held definition of development that focuses almost exclusively on economic indicators. At the global level, the increasing authority of global institutions, and the activities of transnational corporations, suggests that democratic representation and participation are less achievable in the post-Cold War world than many commentators argue. The creation of a global free market, backed by the creation of new global institutions with international standing, described by some as the 'new constitutionalism', favours the interest of capital above the interests of all others. This is seen in the activities of the World Bank, the WTO and regional economic unions, all of which are designed to impose a market discipline that favours corporate and financial interests. Rather than taking a wider view of development that includes human rights, security and dignity, 'new constitutionalism confers privileged rights of citizenship and representation on corporate capital, whilst constraining the democratization process that has involved struggles for representation for hundreds of years' (Gill 1995: 413).

Given the argument that the spread of the democracy idea, as it is currently promoted, relates more to economic growth and development, the interests of global capital and finance and the conditions for globalization, than with human rights and human security, the popular assumption 'if democracy then human rights' is at least questionable.

CHAPTER 5

The Promise of Global Community and Human Rights

The focus of this chapter is the idea of the international citizen, a concept that has gained considerable currency in recent years. The idea of the international citizen is a response to criticisms that globalization leads to less favourable conditions for promoting human rights and human security. It is an attempt to break with the traditional world-view of international relations, which stresses the importance of the rights of states over human rights. Noting the changes in political and social relations characteristic of globalization, proponents of international citizenship argue for the need to develop new forms of citizenship that take full account of new forms of transnational association, short of creating a world government.

At the heart of the historic struggle over legitimate universal human rights are two questions: what kind of rights and who do they benefit? The standard answer to the first question is that lists of legitimate human rights can be found within the pages of international law, and to the second that these rights offer protection to the disempowered, the vulnerable and the weak from governments and other powerful actors. This chapter attempts to examine this standard answer from the perspective of the international political economy. It argues that far from offering protection to those unable to protect themselves, the once subversive idea of human rights is now used to lend legitimacy to the practices of powerful global economic actors. In particular, the emphasis on individualism and limited government, which civil and political freedoms support, has seen the rich accumulate an even greater share of wealth and resources and offered a justification for withdrawing welfare and social entitlements from the poor (Pasha & Blaney 1998).

The argument is conducted in three stages. It begins by briefly reviewing the argument set out in the preceding chapters that the rhetoric of universal human rights is increasingly used to promote both global and domestic economic interests. The definition of human rights adopted by the 'neo-liberal consensus' (Chomsky 1998), which permits this approach, denies the possibility of delivering economic and social rights to excluded groups on the grounds that they are 'unrealistic'. Having established the dominance of a neoliberal view of human rights, the argument goes on to examine the neoliberal rationale for promoting civil and political rights through an examination of the idea of the international citizen. Finally, the argument concludes with a critique that focuses on three aspects of the idea of the international citizen: first, its state-centric character; second, its assumptions about the relationship between state and civil society, and third, assumptions about tolerance.

The Hegemony of Civil and Political Rights

The hegemony of civil and political rights is a theme that runs through all the chapters of this book. As argued in Chapter 3, a set of principles characterizes the dominant image of human rights that supports free market policies, including the recent push to liberalize global trade. Support for an alternative image, which emphasizes economic and social rights, human security and human development, such as that promoted by the United Nations Development Programme (UNDP) (see especially UNDP 1994 and 1999), seems to have evaporated in a post-Cold War order that stresses the importance of the right of the individual to pursue free market economic interests, unfettered by concerns over social consequences. The exercise of these freedoms is reflected in the neoliberal defence of civil and political rights, which argues that for altruistic and pragmatic reasons, the best way to promote human rights is by strengthening trade ties with authoritarian governments (see Chapter 3). In contrast to this, the human rights movement emphasizes the move to a sense of global community, 'one world' politics and a single global history, which globalization is also said to inspire. The growing social movement with an interest in the ecological health of the planet adds further weight to these claims (Bateson 1990).

One of the most recent manifestions of the principle that trade civilizes was seen in the debate within the US over awarding China Permanent Normal Trade Relations (PNTR). Following the pro-democracy incident in Tiananmen Square in 1989, which ended in the death, injury and arrest of many protestors, the US reviewed its trade relations with China annually. Human rights conditions in China were seen as an important element in the review process until 1994, when the Clinton Administration effectively delinked trade issues from the human rights record of trading partners. The proposal to award China PNTR status was criticized by many NGOs who argued that the separation of trade from human rights was a failed experiment because 'every year since "delinkage" human rights conditions in China have gotten worse' (Global Trade Watch 2000). However, drawing on the standard neoliberal view of the relationship between trade and human rights, members of the administration defended PNTR. Typical of this defence is that of US Treasury Secretary, Lawrence H. Summers:

> By learning to 'play by the rules,' both internationally and domestically, China will strengthen the rule of law, which will enable it to become a more reliable partner and a fairer society. It can even lay the groundwork for protection of core values in China, such as human rights, religious freedom, workers' rights and environmental protection. (Summers 2000)

Although the neoliberal consensus accepts the universality and unity of all internationally agreed human rights in formal and legal terms, the political practice of promoting civil and political rights in support of trade and financial liberalization has a long history within the modern human rights regime. We have only to recall that the decision to draft a non-binding Universal *Declaration* of Human Rights, rather than a single legally-binding covenant, was itself a consequence of disagreements between Western countries who sought to prioritize civil and political rights and socialist and less developed countries who favoured economic, social and cultural rights (see Chapter 1; also Evans 1996). With the end of the Cold War, and the increasing pace of globalization, the role of universal human rights seems to have taken a new turn in world politics. Instead of fulfilling its intention of offering protection to the weak and the vulnerable, neoliberal interests have co-opted the idea of human rights as a justification for grabbing 'even more of the world's (and their own nation's) resources than they previously had' and to 'steal back the concessions to social democracy that were forced out of them at the end of the Second World War' (Gearty 1998).

As we shall see in a later section, the increasing numbers of non-state actors have led some authors to the conclusion that a global civil society is already extant. However, such a claim remains unclear. In particular, the significance of other actors can only be assessed in the context of relative power capabilities. For example, while many human rights organizations may have a high profile, and would certainly classify as 'other' actors on the global stage, we should guard against confusing visibility with power and influence (Taylor 1997). On the other hand, the activities of many transnational corporations (TNCs) are less visible, but bring direct consequences for people throughout the world. The investment and production decisions of TNCs, for example, are determined within a global, rather than a national, context to maximize profit.

The global free market in which these corporations operate is not therefore concerned with the traditional boundaries provided by the state or concepts of citizenship. Although in the past it was generally assumed that each state could manage its own national economy, including interventionist policies designed to protect aspects of human security and to provide a welfare safety net for the disadvantaged, the conditions of globalization offer a 24-hour global market that has little concern for national economic planning (Held & McGrew 1993: 270–1). While the deregulation of the global market might be convenient for those who place profit above all other values – a hierarchy that values human worth according to its productive potential – the space for taking human rights and human security seriously is severely constrained (Chomsky 1994).

As argued in Chapter 3, the image of a 'Dutch auction', where states bid against each other to attract investment by offering lower and lower standards of labour, environmental, welfare and social regulation, suggests that the liberalization of trade and finance does not bring benefits to all over time, as neoliberals assert. Evidence of this is seen in the UNDP *Human Development Report* for 1999, which argues that 'the top fifth of the world's people in the richest countries enjoy 82% of the expanding export trade and 68% of foreign direct investment [while] the bottom fifth, barely more than 1%' (UNDP 1999: 31). This sense of exclusion is not confined to the less developed countries. According to the UNDP, more than 35 million people in OECD countries remain unemployed, despite annual growth rates of 2–3% and increases in trade following the Uruguay Round of trade talks (UNDP 1999: 32). Given that the outcome of liberalization brings modes of social exclusion that affect people in both wealthy and poor countries, the idea of global community may be a difficult notion to sustain. However, global community continues to attract considerable interest in some quarters.

International Citizenship

To gain an insight into the move from human rights as protecting the vulnerable to human rights as legitimating the practices of globalization, an examination of the literature on citizenship and the idea of international citizenship is particularly instructive. In proposing the project of the good international citizen, the clear intention is to develop the 'means of weakening the exclusionary character of the modern state and … overcoming an ancient tension between the rights of citizens and duties to the rest of the world' (Linklater 1992: 27), a project that has clear parallels with the post-Second World War project for universal human rights. Making this connection allows the often heard claim that the global human rights regime represents an 'emerging constitution of the world' (Weiss 1994: 30). Although at first reading such notions appear to offer a beguiling solution to the state-citizen vs humanity problem, upon further reflection the project can be seen to offer legitimacy to current practices that continue to deny human rights to the majority of the world's people. Before expanding on this argument some brief outline of the notion of the international citizen is necessary.

A well-known example of this project is Andrew Linklater's essay on the 'good international citizen'. This begins by identifying three generally accepted characteristics that define citizenship: first, 'primary legal rights', which guarantee the freedom of the individual in civil society; second, the 'right to participation in political life', which guarantees the right to take part in government and the exercise of power; and third, 'fundamental duties', which instil an obligation to ameliorate the real inequality that underlies the formal equalities of civil and political rights (Linklater 1992: 23). The substance of these characteristics in any time or place is conditioned by the historic struggles for recognition in which 'both the extent of the citizen body and the nature and extent of citizen rights are constantly contested and changed' (Hutchings 1996: 117). Citizenship should therefore be recognized for its dialectical qualities, which offer an opportunity for excluded groups to challenge the existing order in an effort to 'generate additional claims for change and far-reaching, though not inevitable, patterns of political development' (Linklater 1992: 25). Noting the dialectic of citizenship raises questions concerning the clamour for human rights under conditions of globalization, where the newly emerging structures of the political economy have seen the spread of both great wealth and great poverty, where the decisions and practices of governments, TNCs and international organizations are often decoupled from the reality of many people's lives and experiences, and where new forms of exclusion continue to emerge. However, the task of providing answers to questions of globalization through a re-articulation of citizenship is severely constrained by the widely held assumption that the rights of the citizen cannot be divorced from the particularity of the state. Although the literature accepts that all individuals may possess rights as human beings, emphasis is more usually placed on the 'tragic conflict between citizenship and humanity' (Linklater 1992: 25).

Given these observations, Linklater attempts to reconsider the state-citizen vs humanity question and to offer a solution that navigates a pathway somewhere between the pessimism offered by realists and the optimism of cosmopolitans. In this endeavour, Linklater develops the idea of international citizenship, a citizenship that seeks to undermine the arguments for continuing to legitimate the distinction between 'insiders' and 'outsiders' and thus weaken the exclusionary character of the modern state. Linklater's analysis is interesting but not important to the argument presented here. What is important is Linklater's assertion that

> ... citizenship is not only invoked in defence of old rights, it also plays a prominent role in the continuing effort to affirm and realise new ones. Invoked in this context, citizenship is held to require support for collective action to assist the victims of unjustifiable forms of exclusion anchored in class, ethnicity, gender and race. (Linklater 1992: 22)

Under conditions of globalization the cause, and therefore the resolution, of these exclusionary practices cannot be found solely within the state. Instead, Linklater proposes a system of overlapping citizenship, where the state-citizen, the international citizen and the cosmopolitan citizen exist in harmony and mutual tolerance. According to Linklater, this can be achieved through developing what he takes to be the three dimensions of international citizenship, each of which is loosely equated to the defining characteristics of citizenship outlined earlier.

The first dimension is the collective responsibility of states to maintain order, an order that provides the 'foundation stone upon which more ambitious experiments in good international citizenship might eventually rest' (Linklater 1992: 28). This dimension is central because it acknowledges historic conflicts between states, which must be ameliorated prior to the tasks of developing the international citizen and guaranteeing the freedom of the individual on the global stage. The second dimension of international citizenship concerns respect for other states, including 'upholding international law, relying on diplomacy and seeking to extend the level of consensus between states' (Linklater 1992: 29). Following Hedley Bull, this is a call to develop the institutions of international society, where the rights of the citizen are identified with the rights of states (Bull 1977). The third dimension of international citizenship concerns the right to self-determination. This represents the universal moral principle upon which the tensions between particular and universal claims of citizens' rights rests. The right to self-determination suggests that the 'legitimacy of practices (in domestic politics and international relations) should be decided in the same way: by measures which seek the consent of the included and the excluded' (Linklater 1992: 33–4). Accordingly, all national policy decisions should fulfil the obligation not to take actions that might frustrate the right of others to achieve self-determination.

More recently, Linklater has attempted to develop his notion of a 'post-Westphalian citizenship' in *The Transformation of Political Community* (Linklater 1998). Noting the democratic deficit characteristic of the current era of global politics, where systems of national democracy no longer provide a sense of control over individual and collective lives, and where the decisions of non-accountable international organizations often have greater significance than domestic policy, Linklater calls for a form of citizenship that extends citizen rights 'higher' to international institutions and 'lower' to local institutions. This can be achieved, according to Linklater, by developing the rationalist or international society approach to international politics that takes account of the newly emerging conditions of globalization. Most importantly, Linklater argues that we must 'break with the supposition that national populations have the sovereign right to withhold their consent from any developments within international organizations which clash with their conception of national interest' (Linklater 1998: 192). Although the European Union is held up as an early and, as yet, undeveloped model that includes many of the features of citizenship Linklater has in mind, it is also presented as a model that could eventually encompass the world. Like the Westphalian system of states, which also originated in Europe before embracing the whole of the globe, so too will the new institutions developed in the European Union.

In proposing this project, Linklater attempts to take full account of both the legacy of the previous period, where the state remained the central actor on the international stage, and the new era of globalization, where the individual's identity and loyalty is no longer necessarily tied to the state. Linklater acknowledges that the tensions between the particular and universal claim for rights will not be resolved unless we redefine state-citizenship to include tolerance of multiple loyalties, including those that develop as people engage in greater levels of interaction through non-state institutions and organizations.

Universal Human Rights and International Citizenship

Although the account of international citizenship proposed by Linklater is intended to offer a possible solution to the pressing problems found in a rapidly changing world, any solution that relies upon some notion of citizenship may also offer support for existing practices that are the cause of many human rights violations and much human misery.

Three broad criticisms of the project to promote international citizenship are important to the critique of neoliberal thinking on universal human rights. First, although the central aim in proposing an international citizenship is to find a solution to the state-citizen vs humanity problem, Linklater's project remains largely state-centric. So long as state-citizenship remains integral to developing international citizenship, 'international citizenship appears to depend on the idea of the state-citizen, with other notions of political identity and rights effectively only developing via the *permission* of the state' (Hutchings 1996: 123, original emphasis). This suggests that the rights attached to international citizenship are bestowed from above rather than demanded and developed from below, notwithstanding recent reports of movements organized to resist further globalization in many regions of the world (Inez Ainger 1999; Cheru 1997; Sethi 1997). Given that the idea of international citizenship is in part a response to the demand for greater democracy under conditions of global-ization, conditions that alienate people from existing social institutions, the state-centric focus seems ambiguous (Evans 1997a). On the one hand, proponents argue that new forms of transnational association are stimulated by a desire to re-establish control over political life, following the perceived failure of the state to act in the interests of citizens, while on the other, the state is presented as integral to developing new forms of international political association (Pasha & Blaney 1998: 425).

Moreover, the observation that global politics is now character-ized by a multiplicity of transnational actors, including NGOs, TNCs, international financial institutions and international orga-nizations, is seen by proponents of international citizenship as an exciting and revolutionary phenomenon that demands a new democratic project for global governance. Following this observation, much academic and political energy has been put into proposals that seek to promote democracy within a framework of some kind of global governance in which the state permits the 'development of multiple forms of citizenship' (Linklater 1992: 31). What this project fails to acknowledge, however, is that the development of transnational association generates new forms of loyalty that may not be conducive to new forms of democracy, including the protection of human rights. Indeed, some of the new transnational associations, particularly those concerned with transnational corporations and financial institutions, may actually encourage the very practices that democracy and citizenship are supposed to ameliorate (Thomas 1998). Furthermore, although the idea of citizenship assumes some kind of equality (Tully 1995: 15), civil society is not free of social, political and economic inequalities. By failing to note the undemocratic nature of transnational associational life, and capital's need to maintain inequality, proponents of international citizenship fail to take full account of social and economic power. As Pasha and Blaney have pointed out, most of the recent interest in global democracy and human rights 'does not move our imagination beyond a liberal frame' but, rather, points to 'a failure to attend to the mutually constitutive relationship of civil society, capitalism, and the liberal state', which offers a distorted view of the emancipatory possibilities associated with transnational associational movements (Pasha & Blaney 1998: 419–20).

Those who view the development of new transnational associations as an encouraging indication of the struggle to achieve democracy and the protection of human rights may therefore be criticized for 'romanticizing' the nation state (Luban 1980). For example, Walzer's assertion that state-citizens have the right to choose their own futures through 'authoritative and final' decision-making processes overlooks the possibility that the constitutive processes that stimulated the growth of many transnational associations are the same as those that make the notion of exercising choice through the state less possible (Walzer 1995: 41). That is to say, because people are aware that the state is losing its capability to make meaningful decisions on behalf of citizens, they turn instead to transnational associations as a means of expressing their preferences. As Robert Cox has observed, states are no longer concerned with offering social protection to citizens but, rather, act as agents for delivering the conditions of globalization, by adjusting national policies and practices in accordance with the neoliberal consensus (Cox 1999).

Thus, those who seek to promote democracy and human rights through international citizenship fail to consider the full consequences of the political economy. The choice to develop new international systems of democracy is seen as a political choice, which has no economic context. For example, Linklater's assertion that the European Union is distinguished from other regions of the world by its 'transition from a system of states in which rivalry and suspicion prevail to a more Solidarist society of states and peoples which have become involved in an unusual experiment in transnational *political* cooperation' demonstrates this point (Linklater 1998: 204, emphasis added). In this way, the changing character and capabilities of the state, including the capability to preside over a national economy that attempts to protect weak and vulnerable sections of society, is seen as a political choice, divorced from the global economy and powerful global economic interests.

Furthermore, the state-centric approach to citizenship places the responsibility for promoting human rights onto states through the medium of international law. While acknowledging that the international law approach to promoting human rights remains the central focus of much human rights talk, the emerging conditions of globalization, including the recognition that the authority of the state is undergoing a radical transformation, suggests that implementing substantive international human rights through international law may not produce results (Evans & Hancock 1998). Even when commentators do acknowledge the challenge of globalization, and tacitly recognize that international law has limited potential for guaranteeing human rights, the natural and normal means for protecting human rights remains the creation of international law. In this way human rights becomes a technical issue concerned with agreements and disagreements over the internal logic and elegance of the law, its coherence, extent and meaning. More complex questions to do with efficacy, application and obligations under the particular social, political and economic conditions of globalization are therefore excluded (Young 1989). To expect more of international law overlooks the point that it is itself the product of traditional, state-centric thinking on world politics and cannot therefore resolve the more damaging aspects of an alternative globalized world order (Chimni 1999).

Second, the project for an international citizenship does not avoid the problems that arise in the relationship between the citizen and civil society described by the neoliberal conception of citizenship. Central to these problems is the notion that the neoliberal citizen is 'defended from the state by a series of rights which enable a plurality of ways in which individuals can live their lives within the private sphere of civil society' (Hutchings 1996: 116), thus separating public from private life. In this standard neoliberal interpretation of the state-citizen relationship, the task of protecting the freedom of the individual from interference in the pursuit of economic interests is assigned to the public sphere of the state. Citizenship is therefore concerned with protecting civil and political rights, rights which the state guarantees in the name of the private sphere of civil society. Although in formal terms economic and social rights are often afforded formal parity with civil and political rights, according to the neoliberal conception of citizenship, civil and political rights must be prioritized in order to provide the conditions for wealth creation. Citizens can turn their attention to honouring a duty to support the least fortunate only when these conditions are achieved.

This approach to universal rights has a long history, one that is readily found in the postwar debate on human rights. We need only recall the well-known 'Four Freedoms' speech made by President Roosevelt during 1941, which included the freedom from want, defined to suggest that the claims of the poor and excluded demanded the removal of structural barriers, rather than a redistribution of wealth (Marks 1998).

This is reflected in the general definition of citizenship adopted by neoliberals, which provides for legal *rights* and *rights* of participation but only 'the *duty* to *promote* the widest possible good' (Linklater 1992: 36, emphasis added). While the citizen has the right to seek legal protection if personal and political freedoms are threatened, those suffering economic deprivation have no such rights but must instead rely upon the good faith of duty holders. The duty placed upon the citizen is not even one to *protect* the poor and vulnerable from further violations, a duty that implies positive action, but rather the lesser requirement to *promote* their cause in some indeterminate fashion. Such an approach echoes arguments that have often punctuated debates in the human rights regime developed at the United Nations, for example, the exchanges at Dumbarton Oaks and San Francisco over whether the United Nations Charter itself should call for the promotion or protection of human rights and the prolonged debates during preparation for the Covenant on Economic, Social and Cultural Rights over the distinction between rights and duties (Evans 1996). Furthermore, fostering a duty to promote human rights in the interests of the widest possible good tends to reinforce the centrality of the individual in the human rights debate at the expense of structural causes of violations. Current practices that are the cause of many human rights violations – practices that are legitimated by neoliberal freedoms exercised within existing structures – are marginalized and are less likely to present a challenge to the dominant value system (Salmi 1993; Galtung 1994).

These criticisms suggest that the attempt to secure universal civil, political and economic rights through the medium of citizenship may, in fact, reinforce a set of values that support current exclusionary practices found in globalization. Notwithstanding the addition of duties as well as rights in the modern interpretation of citizenship, the idea of the international citizen does not offer a convincing argument for securing human rights in the age of globalization. It fails because it confuses the rights of the individual with the rights of the citizen and does not take full account of the relationship between civil society, the state and the citizen.

How then does the individual claiming universal human rights differ from the citizen claiming the rights of citizenship? In his essay 'On the Jewish Question', Marx argues that civil society holds the key to this question. For Marx 'the so-called human rights, the rights of *droits de l'homme* in contrast to *droits de citoyen*, are nothing but the rights of members of civil society' (Marx 1994: 44). Since civil society represents the private sphere, a sphere intended to guarantee the liberty necessary to pursue private satisfactions, human rights are concerned with the egoistic, atomized, isolated individual, separated from community. The exercise of human rights in civil society is therefore concerned with rights to enjoy and dispose of property arbitrarily, free of all social or political responsibilities, except those commensurate with the equal rights of others (Marx 1994: 45). In such a society, a society where the individual is free to exploit others and is encouraged to do so, the possibility of developing the necessary emotional ties associated with community are severely constrained: community and exploitation are incompatible (van de Pijl 1997). None the less, to maintain social order there remains a need to create an imaginary space, the state, in which to fabricate the institutions of unity, including those associated with equality, democracy and citizenship (Furet 1984: 16–18). Human rights therefore offer support for the egoistic individual, withdrawn into private interests and separated from community. All that is left to hold people together is 'natural necessity, need and private interests, the conservation of their property and their egoistic person' (Marx 1994: 46).

This interpretation of civil society constitutes relations between public and private spheres that offer a unique opportunity for new forms of social power. This social power is located in the legitimation of rights, which are claimed by individuals as members of civil society. As expressed by Ellen Meiksins Wood, civil society represents 'a particular network of social relations which does not simply stand in opposition to the coercive, "policing" and "administrative" functions of the state but represents the *relocation* of these functions, or at least some significant part of them' (Meiksins Wood 1995: 254, original emphasis). The role of the state is to oversee the existing order, to act as 'nightwatchman' for guaranteeing 'fair play' and the 'rules of the game', rather than to initiate change, which is the role of civil society (Gramsci 1996: 262–3). All thought of transforming civil society through the formal political processes represented by the state is illusory (Furet 1984: 15). Although the image of the state as the guardian of individual human rights continues to be widely shared – including the image of the state acting as the agent of civil society in fulfilling the citizen's duty to deal with unacceptable inequalities – in this reading of civil society the state is more concerned with property, appropriation, exploitation and securing the domination of particular economic interests and acts accordingly to protect the violation of these values. In short, the separation of public from private life, politics from economics and the state from civil society provides a context where 'political emancipation emancipates civil society from politics and opens the way for the unfettered materialism of interests' (Furet 1984: 19).

The human rights associated with neoliberal civil society are limited to civil and political claims, claims that secure a sphere of freedom in which the egoistic individual pursues economic interests. If some groups choose to use the freedoms offered by civil society to challenge, say, the class, gender, ethnic or race inequalities underlying the formal equalities of citizenship, the state intervenes, in most cases within the implementational constraints of a system of law or, if this fails, through direct action by the police and military (Collins 1990). When such events do occur, civil society attempts to negate that which it has produced by appeal to the state to defend the existing order. To paraphrase Marx, the rights represented by civil society are extended to those who want to receive the freedom of property or the egoism of trade, not to those who desire to free themselves from property and trade. The role of political life is to secure the purpose of civil society, which is the separation of the egoistic individual from the community, to secure the individual's liberty in the private sphere and to legitimate the suppression of any challenge to an order that supports the economic interests of the dominant group. In short, it is civil society that constitutes the limits, form and extent of rights, not the state. To elevate economic 'aspirations' to the level of rights threatens core neoliberal values and the whole purpose of the postwar human rights regime, which is to gain legitimation for free market, *laissez-faire* practices and the expansion of the neoliberal economy on a global scale.

The conclusions to be drawn from this analysis suggest that the protection of human rights, particularly economic and social rights, cannot be achieved through mechanisms associated with the state, international law and the idea of the international citizen. Indeed, far from offering a satisfactory response to globalization, the idea of the international citizen lends further support to neoliberal assertions that economic and social claims are aspirations not universal human rights. In short, the vacuum left by the decline of the state as the main, if not the only, political actor in world politics, is not filled by civil society. Rather, civil society reflects the narrow self-interests of those in a structural position to take full advantage of the conditions of globalization, to the exclusion of the many (Pasha & Blaney 1998: 432).

Third, proponents of civil society and citizenship acknowledge that the new 'politics of recognition demands new expressions of sensitivity to difference and new possibilities for expanding the range of permissible disagreements' (Linklater 1998: 187). This is the virtue of tolerance, which is a fundamental principle of social pluralism. However, proponents of civil society do not intend that tolerance should be extended to all groups, ideas and values. Instead, tolerance is extended to those who accept the general purposes of civil society by adopting its values and following the 'correct' procedures for realizing their particular vision of the 'good life'. Those who attempt to challenge the general principles of the dominant economic, social and political order are tolerated only in so far as they 'do not seek to make the transition from word to deed, from speech to action' (Marcuse 1969: 85–6). In Marcuse's view, this produces the condition of 'repressive tolerance', which is little more than a 'market-place of ideas' in which notions of the 'good life' compete for attention within the confines of a particular version of civil society (Marcuse 1969: 110). However:

> The norms of behaviour demanded of members of civil society are dedicated to preserving this economic, cultural, and ideological marketplace. Thus, the inequalities of liberal civil society are depoliticized, despite the serious social consequences of such inequality. The individual who enters these civil spaces is expected to adopt a certain stance towards his or her own person and towards others. (Pasha & Blaney 1998: 423)

Those perceived as a threat to the principles manifest in civil society are marginalized, either by labelling them 'mad' and therefore not worthy of 'rational' consideration (Keeley 1990) or by mobilizing official violence if that fails.

Tolerance and civility are therefore concerned with the preservation and management of a particular form of civil society, a narrowing of the political agenda and the exclusion of actors whose voices appear as a threat. In neoliberal societies, tolerance is practised by legitimating a set of civil liberties and freedoms that are granted to all citizens, regardless of 'race, colour, sex, language, religion, political or other opinion, national or social origin, property, birth or other status' (UDHR Art. 2). Against this expression of formal equality and tolerance, however, is the actual practice of tolerance, which cannot be divorced from power relations that determine what will or will not be tolerated. For Marcuse, in the face of repressive tolerance and inequality 'the idea of available alternatives evaporates into an utterly utopian dimension' unless society is free of 'indoctrination', 'manipulation' and 'extraneous authority' (Marcuse 1969: 92–3).

An example of repressive tolerance operating at the global level can be seen in the treatment of new states following decolonization. Although the imperial powers withdrew from these countries, thereby removing the immediate threat of coercion if colonial peoples resisted the spread of globalization or failed to embrace the principles of a market economy, self-determination did not mean autonomy. Rather, self-determination meant freedom to embrace the rules, norms and principles of the emerging neoliberal global order. That these rules and norms often lead to human rights violations, for example, by threatening economic, social and cultural life, denying the right to join a trade union or the right to sustenance, is rarely acknowledged and often tolerated in the name of 'progress' (Evans 1999). To repeat, for the neoliberal consensus, the 'high transition costs' of economic growth and development are a price worth paying for future benefits. Put succinctly by Marcuse, progress towards tolerance is 'perhaps more than before asserted by violence and suppression on a global scale', when tolerance is extended to 'policies, conditions, and modes of behaviour which should not be tolerated because they are impeding, if not destroying, the chances of creating an existence without fear and misery' (Marcuse 1969: 82). Tolerance may therefore perform the task of 'closure' by excluding alternatives that threaten the existing order, for example, by defining peace in terms of the preparation for war or human rights as a legal problem rather than one best understood within the context of the political economy.

Conclusion

Linklater's attempt to develop the idea of the good international citizen has already gained wide acceptance (Carter 1997; Nossal 1998; Wheeler & Dunne 1998). Although further attempts to develop and operationalize the concept exhibit detailed differences, they are all concerned with understanding democracy and human rights within the context of a changing world order. However, as this book has attempted to demonstrate, the idea of the international citizen is not unproblematic and, in its current conceptualization, may not deliver the outcomes that proponents seek. The argument here is not that some form of citizenship cannot lend support to protecting human rights but, rather, that it cannot be done unless the critical points raised here are accommodated. In short, the success of the project to develop the idea of the international citizen depends upon our ability to understand the current configuration of social forces, forms of state and world order (Cox 1981), which seems to be lacking in much of the literature. For example, although Linklater is well known for his work on critical theory, his proposal has no clear theory of history that allows us to understand the processes of change that will eventually lead to international citizenship and the protection of human rights (Hoffman 1988). Therefore, the relationship between the project for an international citizenship and the present order remains unclear.

This chapter set out to investigate how the idea of universal human rights was co-opted by the prevailing neoliberal consensus in support of processes associated with globalization. Civil and political rights form the core of neoliberal values upon which free market, *laissez-faire* economics are based. Through an examination of the idea of the international citizen, it was argued that the attempt to introduce a duty to promote the widest possible social good falls far short of an obligation to respond to claims for economic and social rights. Indeed, while proponents of the idea of the international citizen might claim to be responding to the global political economy, it serves only to obfuscate important facets of the human rights debate. Those who stand in the way of the 'imperatives' of globalization risk violations of their rights, both civil and political and economic and social.

As the state moves from being an active policy maker to a passive unit of administration, there is a decline in the capacity of people to participate in defining a political agenda that expresses a genuine concern for human rights and human dignity. With the realization that the global rather than the national economy exercises greater influence on economic well-being and the prospects for rights, the state loses its significance as a centre of authority through which people can express their preferences. Instead, the focus turns to international institutions and transnational organizations that have few democratic credentials, although they assume the task of providing the rules for action. In response to the new social formations that are characteristic of globalization, international citizenship seeks a pathway to promoting human rights. However, the discussion offered here suggests that the current project ends by giving greater legitimacy to practices that are the cause of human rights violations.

CONCLUSION

The Process of Human Rights

This book has attempted to analyse and critique some of the issues that surround the project to protect universal human rights, first begun at the end of the Second World War. Other issues could have included environmental rights, and the feminist critique that the human rights regime is not gender neutral (Peterson & Parisi 1998). At the centre of the arguments presented here are questions to do with what kind of rights dominate the human rights agenda and who benefits from the project to promote human rights? In answer to the first question, it was argued that the dominant image of human rights remains that of civil and political rights and, to the second, that these rights offer legitimation for particular forms of social activity that support the interests of the neoliberal consensus. However, under conditions of globalization, which offer greater possibilities for raising people's awareness to their human rights and for exposing human rights abuses, the potential for sustaining an image of rights that support particular interests is severely strained.

The rapid changes in social, political and economic relations characteristic of globalization, subject people to a dynamic global culture that accelerates processes of inclusion and exclusion. These processes challenge existing cultural knowledge that defines the 'self' in opposition to the other, a phenomenon that is most intensively experienced in postcolonial countries (Wilson 1997). In response, people attempt to assert their individuality within the wider context of humanity, often through claiming universal human rights. However, for those most in need, dominant images of human rights offer little by way of comfort. At the beginning of the twenty-first century, the lack of consensus on the moral case for understanding pernicious inequalities as a human rights issue, and therefore the case for reforming international economic structures to achieve a measure of social justice, seems remote. Although the formal measures undertaken at the United Nations continue to provide a focus for all activities associated with the protection of human rights, the agenda of world politics fails to take the link between inequality and human rights seriously (Woods 1999).

The year 2000 annual meeting of the United Nations Commission for Human Rights confirms this assertion. Most of the debate centred on civil and political rights to the exclusion of economic, social and cultural rights, reflecting the Commission's continued focus on 'gross' violations of human rights associated with war, civil war and authoritarian regimes. The violence associated with structural causes of human rights abuses, where the relationship between the abused and the abuser is less clear and where abuses provide less dramatic images, seems to attract little attention. Further evidence of the success of the neoliberal consensus in defining the limits of rights, was seen at the press conference attended by Mary Robinson, the United Nations Commissioner for Human Rights. During that press conference, not one question was asked 'about the right of the silent majority of suffering human beings – close to half the world's population for whom life is a daily struggle for survival and for whom these concepts of rights may seem remote' (Singh 2000: 40). As tellingly, Robinson stressed the need to pursue those responsible for civil and political violations, while the challenge of economic violations demanded only that we 'keep human rights at the forefront of strategies for governance' (quoted in Singh 2000: 41).

None of the arguments presented here should, however, be understood as denying the importance of human rights in pursuit of human security. Neither should they be understood as the counsel of despair. The historic struggle for rights suggests that human rights are better understood as a process rather than an endpoint. To sit passively, and accept uncritically that the programmes and actions undertaken by the United Nations are necessarily directed at guaranteeing human security, overlooks the complex relationship between power and rights and ignores the need to engage in the process. Furthermore, the tendency to move from observing human rights problems to creating solutions, ignoring the intermediate steps of analysis and reflection, leads to replicating the errors of the past, a wasteful use of scarce resources and a pessimism generated by disappointment.

Bibliography

Acosta, Mariclare (1992), 'The Democratization Process in Mexico: A Human Rights Issue', in John Cavanagh et al. (eds), *Trading Freedom: How Free Trade Affects Our Lives, Work and Environment*, San Francisco, Institute of Food Development Policy, 82–5.

Addo, M.K. (1987), 'The Implications for Some Aspects of Contemporary International Economic Law on International Human Rights Law', unpublished PhD thesis, Essex.

Adeola, F.O. (2000), 'Cross-National Environmental Injustice and Human Rights Issues – A Preview of Evidence in the Developing World', *American Behavioural Scientist*, 43:4, 686–706.

Alston, Philip (1994), 'The UN's Human Rights Record: From San Francisco to Vienna and Beyond', *Human Rights Quarterly*, 16:2, 375–90.

Alston, Philip (1996), 'Labor rights provisions in US trade law: Aggressive unilateralism?', in Lance A. Compon and Stephen F. Diamond (eds), *Human Rights, Labor Rights, and International Trade*, Philadelphia, University of Pennsylvania Press.

Amin, Samir (1997), 'The State and Development', in David Held (ed.), *Political Theory Today*, Cambridge, Polity, 305–29.

Arat, Zeha (1991), *Democracy and Human Rights in Developing Countries*, London, Lynne Rienner.

Arrigo, Linda Gail (1993), 'A View from the United Nations Conference on Human Rights, Vienna, June 1993', *Bulletin of Concerned Asian Scholars*, 25:3, 69–72.

Augelli, Enrico and Graig Murphy (1988), *America's Quest and the Third World*, London, Pinter.

Barber, M. and R. Grainne (eds) (1993), *Damning the Three Gorges*, second edition, London, Earthscan.

Barkun, Michael (1968), *Law Without Sanction*, London, Yale University Press.

Bateson, Mary Catherine (1990), 'Beyond Sovereignty: An Emerging Global Community', in R.B.J. Walker and Saul H. Mendlowitz (eds), *Contesting Sovereignty: Redefining Political Community,* Boulder, Lynne Rienner.

Beetham, David (1992), 'Liberal Democracy and the Limits of Democratization', *Political Studies*, XL, 40–53.

Beitz, Charles (1983), 'Economic Rights and Distributive Justice in Developing Societies', *World Politics*, 33:3, 321–45.

Bentham, Jeremy (1957), quoted in Maurice Cranston, 'Human rights: real and supposed', in D.D. Raphael (ed.), *Political Theory and the Rights of Man*, London, Macmillan.

Berting, Jan (1993), 'Technological impact on human rights: Models of development, science and technology, and human rights', in C.G. Weeramantry (ed.), *The Impact of Technology on Human Rights: Global Case Studies*, Tokyo, UN University Press, 13–44.

Bhatnager, Bhuvan (1992), 'Participation Development and the World Bank: Opportunities and Concerns', in Bhuvan Bhatnager (ed.), *Participatory Development and the World Bank*, World Bank Report, Washington DC, 13–30.

Borosage, Robert (1997), 'Fast Track to Nowhere', *The Nation*, 20, September, 20–22.

Boyle, James (1985), 'Ideas and Things: International Legal Scholarship and the Prisonhouse of Language', *Harvard International Law Journal*, 26:2, 327–59.

Boyle, K. (1995), 'Stock Taking on Human Rights: The Conference on Human Rights Vienna 1993', *Political Studies*, 43, 79–95.

Bull, Hedley (1977), *The Anarchical Society*, Basingstoke, Macmillan.

Burrell, Ian (1998), 'The P&O port that no one wants', *Independent on Sunday*, 1 February, 10.

Buzan, B. et al. (1993), *The Logic of Anarchy*, New York, Columbia University Press.

Caballero-Anthony, M. (1995), 'Human Rights, Economic Change and Political Development', in J.T.H. Tang (ed.), *Human Rights and International Relations in the Asian Pacific*, London, Pinter.

Cafruny, A.W. (1989), 'Economic Conflicts and the Transformation of the Atlantic Order', in S. Gull (ed.), *Atlantic Relations: Beyond the Reagan Era*, New York, St. Martin's Press.

Camilleri, Joseph (1990), 'Rethinking Sovereignty in a Shrinking, Fragmented World', in R.B.J. Walker and Saul Mendlovitz (eds), *Contending Sovereignties*, Boulder, Lynne Rienner, 13–44.

Carlin, John (1998), 'What's a deal among friends?', *Independent on Sunday*, 19 April.

Carothers, Thomas (1994), 'Democracy and human rights: Policy allies or rivals?', *The Washington Quarterly*, 17:3, 109–20.

Carr, E.H. (1939), *The Twenty Years' Crisis*, London, Macmillan.

Carter, A. (1997), 'Nationalism and Global Citizenship', *Australian Journal of Politics and History*, 43:1, 67–81.

Cassese, Antonio (1990), *Human Rights in a Changing World*, Oxford, Oxford University Press.

Chatterjee, Pratap, and Matthias Finger (1994), *The Earth Brokers: Power, Politics and World Development*, London, Routledge.

Cheru, Fantu (1997), 'The Silent Revolution and the Weapons of the Weak: Transformation and Innovation from Below', in Stephen Gill and James Mittelman (eds), *Innovation and Transformation in International Studies*, Cambridge, Cambridge University Press, 153–68.

Chimni, B.S. (1999), 'Marxism and International Law', *Economic and Political Weekly*, 34:6, 337–49.

Chinkin, Christine (1998), 'International Law and Human Rights', in Tony Evans (ed.), *Human Rights Fifty Years On: A Reappraisal*, Manchester, Manchester University Press.

Chomsky, Noam (1978), *Human Rights and American Foreign Policy*, Nottingham, Spokesman Books

Chomsky, Noam (1992), 'World Order and Its Rules: Variations on Some Themes', *Journal of Law and Society*, 20:2, 145–65.

Chomsky, Noam (1994), *World Orders, Old and New*, London, Pluto.

Chomsky, Noam (1998), 'The United States and the Challenge of Relativity', in Tony Evans (ed.), *Human Rights Fifty Years On: A Reappraisal*, Manchester, Manchester University Press, 26–56.

Christian Aid (1996), *After the Prawn Rush: the Human and Environmental costs of Commercial Prawn Farming*, Christian Aid report, 11 May.

Christian Aid (1997), *A Sporting Chance*, Christian Aid report, March.

Christian Aid (1999), *Fair Shares? Transnational Companies, the WTO and the World's Poorest Communities*, Christian Aid report.

Clark, Ian (1999), *Globalization and International Relations Theory*, Oxford, Oxford University Press.

Collins, Hugh (1990), *Marxism and Law*, Oxford, Oxford University Press.

Conley, M. and D. Livermore (1996), 'Human Rights, Development and Democracy: The Linkage Between Theory and Practice', *Canadian Journal of Development Studies*, No. XIXI, 19–26.

Coote, Belinda (1996), *The Trade Trap: Poverty and the Global Commodity Market*, Oxford, Oxfam.

Cox, Robert W. (1981), 'Social Forces, States and World Orders: Beyond International Relations Theory', *Millennium*, 10:2, 126–55.

Cox, Robert W. (1994), 'The Crisis of World Order and the Challenge of International Organization', *Conflict and Cooperation*, 29:2, 99–114.

Cox, Robert W. (1995), 'A Perspective on Globalization', in James H. Mittelman (ed.), *Globalization: Critical Reflections*, Boulder, Lynne Rienner, 21–30.

Cox, Robert W. (1997), 'Democracy in Hard Times: Economic Globalization and the Limits to Liberal Democracy', in Anthony Mcgrew (ed.), *The Transformation of Democracy*, Cambridge, Polity Press, 49–75.

Cox, Robert W. (1999), 'Civil Society at the Turn of the Millennium: Prospects for an Alternative World Order', *Review of International Studies*, 25:1, 2–28.

Cranston, Maurice (1973), *What Are Human Rights?*, London, Bodley Head.

Cranston, Maurice (1983), 'Are there any human rights?', *Daedalus*, 112:4, 1–18.

Crow, Roger (1998), 'Shell to come clean and go green', *Guardian*, 11 March.

Dalby, Simon (1992), 'Security, Modernity, Ecology: The Dilemma of the Post-Cold War Discourse', *Alternatives*, vol. 17, 95–134.

Daly, E. (1997), 'Time for Justice to be Done', *Independent on Sunday*, 6 July, 17.

Danilenko, Geunady (1991), 'The Changing Structure of the International Community: Constitutional Imperatives', *Harvard Journal of International Law*, 32:2, 353–61.

Davis, Michael C. (1998), 'The Price of Rights: Constitution and East Asian Economic Development', *Human Rights Quarterly*, 20:2, 303–37.

Declaration on the Right to Development (1986), GA res. 41/128, UN Doc. A/41/53.

Dichter, Thomas (1992), 'Demystifying Popular Participation: International Mechanisms for Popular Participation', in Bhuvan Bhatnagar and Audrey C. Williams (eds), *Participatory Development and the World Bank*, Washington, World Bank Report, 89–95.

Donnelly, Jack (1986), 'International Human Rights: A Regime Analysis', *International Organization*, 40:3, 599–642.

Donnelly, Jack (1989a), *Universal Human Rights in Theory and Practice*, Ithaca, Cornell University Press.

Donnelly, Jack (1989b), 'Repression and development: The political contingency of human rights trade-offs', in David P. Forsythe (ed.), *Human Rights and Development*, Basingstoke, Macmillan, 305–28.

Donnelly, Jack (1993), *International Human Rights*, Boulder, Westview Press.

Donnelly, Jack (1994), 'Human Rights in the New World Order', *World Policy Review*, 9:2, 249–77.

Economist (1993), 'The Red and the Blue', 8 May, 22.

Ehrenberg, Kaniel S. (1996), 'From intentions to action: An ILO-GATT/WTO enforcement regime for international labor rights', in Lance A. Compa and Stephen F. Diamond (eds), *Human Rights, Labour Rights, and International Trade*, Philadelphia, University of Pennsylvania Press, 163–80.

Eisenhower, Dwight D. (1963), *The White House Years: Mandate for Change – 1953–56*, London, Heinemann.

Evans, Tony (1995), 'US Hegemony, Domestic Politics and the Project for Universal Human Rights', *Statecraft and Diplomacy*, 6:3, 314–41.

Evans, Tony (1996), *US Hegemony and the Project of Universal Human Rights*, Basingstoke, Macmillan.

Evans, Tony (1997a), 'Democracy and Universal Human Rights', in Anthony McGrew (ed.), *Democracy in Transition*, Cambridge, Polity Press.

Evans, Tony (1997b), 'Universal Human Rights: Imposing Values', in Caroline Thomas and Peter Wilkin (eds), *Globalisation and the South*, Basingstoke, Macmillan, 90–105.

Evans, Tony (1998), *Human Rights Fifty Years On: A Reappraisal*, Manchester, Manchester University Press.

Evans, Tony (1999), 'Trading Human Rights', in Annie Taylor and Caroline Thomas (eds), *Global Trade and Global Social Issues*, London, Routledge, 31–52.

Evans, Tony and Jan Hancock (1998), 'Doing Something Without Doing Anything: International Human Rights Law and the Challenge of Globalization', *Journal of International Human Rights*, 2:3, 1–21.

Evans, Tony and Peter Wilson (1992), 'International Regimes and the English School of International Relations', *Millennium: Journal of International Relations*, 22:1, 329–51.

Falk, Richard (1980), 'The Theoretical Foundations of Human Rights', in R.P. Newburg (ed.), *The Politics of Human Rights*, New York, New York University Press.

Falk, Richard (1981), *Human Rights and State Sovereignty*, London, Holmes and Meier.

Fatic, Aleksander (2000), *Reconciliation via the War Crimes Tribunal?*, Oxford, Ashgate.

Felice, William (1999), 'The Viability of the United Nations Approach to Economic and Social Human Rights in a Global Economy', *International Affairs*, 75:3, 563–98.

Femia, Joseph (1987), *Gramsci's Political Thought: Hegemony, Consciousness and the Revolutionary Process*, Oxford, Clarendon Press.

Flinchum, Robin (1998), 'Women's Resistance in Chiapas', *Third World Resurgence*, No. 95, 35–6.

Fox, George H. and George Nolte (1995), 'Intolerant Democracies', *American Journal of International Law*, 36:1, 1–70.

Frank, Thomas (1988), 'The Emerging Right to Democratic Government', *American Journal of International Law*, 86, 45–91.

Freeman, Michael (1995), 'Human Rights: Asia and the West', in James T.H. Tang (ed.), *Human Rights and International Relations in the Asia-Pacific*, London, Pinter, 13–24.

Freeman, Michael (1996), 'Human Rights, Democracy and "Asian Values"', *Pacific Review*, 9:3, 352–66.

Fukuyama, Francis (1989), 'The End of History', *The National Interest*, Summer, 3–18.

Furet, François (1984), *Marx and the French Revolution*, London, University of Chicago Press.

Galtung, Johan (1994), *Human Rights in Another Key*, Cambridge, Polity Press.

Ganesan, Arvid (1998), 'Partners in Crime', *Guardian* (Society supplement), 20 May, 4.

Gearty, Connor (1998), 'No Human Rights Please, We're Capitalists', *Independent On Sunday* (Culture supplement), 13 December, 34.

George, Susan (1999), *The Lucano Report*, London, Pluto.

Giddens, Anthony (1990), *Modernity and Self-Identity*, Cambridge, Polity Press.

Giddens, Anthony (1992), *The Consequences of Modernity*, Cambridge, Cambridge University Press.

Gill, Stephen (1995), 'Globalization, Market Civilisation, and Disciplinary Neoliberalism', *Millennium: Journal of International Studies*, 24:3, 399–423.

Gill, Stephen (1996), 'Globalization, Democratization and Indifference', in James H. Mittelman (ed.), *Globalization: Critical Reflections*, Boulder, Lynne Rienner, 105–28.

Gills, Barry (1995), 'Whither Democracy? Globalization and the New Hellenism', paper given at the annual conference of the British International Studies Association, Southampton.

Gills, Barry, J. Rocamora and R. Wilson (1993), *Low Intensity Democracy: Power in the New World Order*, London, Pluto.

Gingrich, Newt (1998), Interview for *Human Rights and Democracy*, Public Broadcasting Service <www.pbs.org.globalization>.

Global Trade Watch (2000), Talking points <www.citizens.org/pctrade/china/talkingpts>.

Gramsci, Antonio (1996), *Selections from the Prison Notebook*, Quinton Hoare and Geoffrey Smith (eds), London, Lawrence and Wisehart.

Grotius, Hugo (1964), *De Jure Belli ac Pacis Libri Tres*, London, Wildy and Sons.

Guardian (1998), 'Misery for Migrant Millions', 7 January, 1.

Guardian (1999), 'Former UN Official Decries Sanctions on Iraq,' 27 January, 13.

Haas, Ernst B. (1970), *The Web of Interdependence*, Englewood Cliffs, NJ, Prentice Hall.

Hansenne, M. (1996), 'International Trade and Labour Standards: The Director General of the ILO Speaks Out', *International Labour Review*, 135:2, 230–8.

Held, David (1987), *Models of Democracy*, Cambridge, Polity Press.

Held, David (1991), 'Democracy and the Global System', in David Held (ed.), *Political Theory Today*, Cambridge, Polity, 297–325.

Held, David (1992), 'Democracy: From City State to Cosmopolitan Order', *Political Studies*, Vol. XL (special issue), 10–39.

Held, David (1995), *Democracy and the Global Order*, Cambridge, Polity.

Held, David and Anthony McGrew (1993), 'Globalization and the Liberal Democratic State', *Government and Opposition*, 28:2, 161–88.

Held, David and Anthony McGrew (1999), *Global Transformation*, Cambridge, Polity Press.

Hendrick, James (undated), Papers of Eleanor Roosevelt, Roosevelt Library, Hyde Park, New York, Box No. 4587.

Henkin, Louis (1995), 'US Ratifications of Human Rights Conventions: The Ghost of Senator Bricker', *American Journal of International Law*, 89:2, 341–50.

Herrmann, Pauline (1993), 'Human Environmental Crisis and the Transnational Corporation: The Question of Culpability', *Human Ecology*, 23:2, 285–89.

Hertz, John H. (1954), 'The Rise and Demise of the Territorial State', *World Politics*, 9:4, 473–93.

Hindess, Barry (1991), 'Imaginary Presuppositions of Democracy', *Economy and Society*, 20:2, 173–95.

Hindess, Barry (1992), 'Power and Rationality: The Western Conception of Political Community', *Alternatives*, 17, 149–63.

Hindess, Barry (1999), 'Representation Ingrafted Upon Democracy', Annual Hanna Arendt Lecture, University of Southampton, June 1999.

Hirst, Paul and Grahame Thompson (1996), *Globalization in Question?*, Cambridge, Polity Press.

Hoffman, Mark (1987), 'Critical Theory and the Inter-paradigm Debate', *Millennium: Journal of International Studies*, 16:2, 231–49.

Hoffman, Mark (1988), 'States, Cosmopolitanism and Normative International Theory', *Paradigms*, 2:1, 60–75.

Hoffman, S. (1977), 'The Hell of Good Intentions', *Foreign Policy*, 29, 3–26.

Holman, F.E. (1952), 'Giving America Away', *Vital Speeches of the Day*, 16, 1 October, 748–53.

Holman, F.E. (1953), 'The Greatest Threat to Our American Heritage', *Vital Speeches of the Day*, 24, 15 December, 711–17.

Hormats, Robert (1998), Interview for *Globalization and Human Rights*, Public Broadcasting Service <www.pbs.org.globalization>.

HRW (Human Rights Watch) (1995), *The Ogoni Crisis: A Case Study of Military Repression in South East Nigeria*, HRW Report, July.

HRW (Human Rights Watch) (1996), 'No Guarantees: Sex Discrimination in Mexico's Maquiladora Sector', *Human Rights Watch Women's Rights Project*, 8:6(B).

HRW (Human Rights Watch) (1999), 'Human Rights and Democracy in Latin America and the Caribbean', Paper prepared for the Heads of State and governments of the European Union, Latin America and the Caribbean, Rio de Janeiro, June 1999.

Human Rights Committee (1994), 52nd meeting, Doc. CCPR/C/21/rev.1/add.6.

Humphrey, John (1984), *Human Rights and the United Nations: The Great Adventure*, Dobbs Ferry, Transnational Publishers.

Hutchings, Kimberly (1996), 'The Idea of International Citizenship', in Barry Holden (ed.), *The Ethical Dimensions of Global Change*, Basingstoke, Macmillan.

Huymans, Jef (1995), 'Post-Cold War Implosion and Globalisation: Liberalism Running Past Itself', *Millennium: Journal of International Studies*, 24:3, 471–87.

Ikenberry, G. J. and C.A. Kupchan (1990), 'Socialization and Hegemonic Power', *International Organization*, 44:5, 283–315.

ILO (International Labour Organisation) (1996), *World Employment 1996/97: National Policies in a Global Market*, Geneva, ILO.

Inez Ainger, Katharine (1999), 'In India, Peasants are Burning Crops, Mocking their Leaders – and Dying. Here's Why ...', *Guardian* (Society supplement), 27 January, 4–5.

Jackson, Robert (1990), 'Martin Wight, International Theory and the Good Life', *Millennium: Journal of International Relations*, 19:2, 261–72.

Johansen, Robert C. (1993), 'Military Policies and the State System as Impediments to Democracy', in David Held (ed.), *Prospects for Democracy: North, South, East and West*, Cambridge, Polity Press.

Johnston, Barbara Rose and Gregory Button (1994), 'Human Environmental Rights Issues and the Multinational Corporation: Industrial Development in the Free Trade Zone', in Barbara Rose Johnston, (ed.), *Who Pays the Price?*, Washington, Island Press.

Juniper, Tony (1999), 'Unfair Trade Sparks New World War', *Guardian*, 17 August, 14.

Kaplan, M.A. and N.B. Katzenback (1961), *The Politics and Foundations of International Law*, London, John Wylie.

Kaufman, N.G. and D. Whiteman (1988), 'Opposition to Human Rights Treaties in the United States: The Legacy of the Bricker Amendment', *Human Rights Quarterly*, 10:3, 309–37.

Keeley, James (1990), 'Towards a Foucauldian Analysis of International Regimes', *International Organization*, 44:1, 83–105.

Kennan, George (1985), 'Morality and Foreign Policy', *International Affairs*, 64:2, 205–18.

Keohane, Robert O. (1984), *After Hegemony: Co-operation and Discord in the World Political Economy*, Princeton, Princeton University Press.

Khor, Martin (2000), Speech to the World Economic Forum, Davos, Switzerland, 28 January <www.twnside.org.sg>.

Kirkpatrick, Jeanne (1982), 'Dictatorship and Double Standards', in H.J. Wiarda (ed.), *Human Rights and US Human Rights Policy*, Washington DC, American Enterprises Institute.

Kothari, Miloon (1998), Oral statement delivered to the United Nations Sub-Commission on Prevention of Discrimination and Protection of Minorities, Geneva, 12 August.

Kotheri, Smitu (1994), 'Global Economic Insitutions and Democracy: A View From India', in J. Cavanagh, D. Wysham and M. Arrunda (eds), *Beyond Bretton Woods*, London, Pluto Press, 39–54.

Krasner, Stephen (ed.) (1983), *International Regimes*, London, Cornell University Press.

Kudryartsev, V.N. (1986), 'Human rights and the Soviet Constitution', in *Philosophical Foundations of Human Rights*, New York, UNESCO.

Lawyers Committee for Human Rights (1989), *Human Rights and US Foreign Policy: United States Policy Towards South Africa*, New York, Lawyers Committee for Human Rights.

Lawyers Committee for Human Rights (1992a), *Human Rights and US Foreign Policy*, New York, Lawyers Committee for Human Rights.

Lawyers Committee for Human Rights (1992b), Letter to Senator Claiborne Pell, *Human Rights Law Journal*, 14, 3–5.

Lee, E. (1996), 'Globalization and Employment: Is Anxiety Justified?', *International Labour Review*, 135:5, 485–97.

LeQuesne, Caroline (1996), *Reforming World Trade: The Social and Environmental Priorities*, Oxford, Oxfam.

Lerch, Charles O. (1965), *The Cold War ... and After*, Englewood Cliffs, NJ, Prentice Hall.

Lewis, Michael (1998), 'The money world bows to American bullies', *Independent on Sunday*, 3 May, 6.

Linklater, Andrew (1990), 'The Problem of Community in International Relations', *Alternatives*, Vol. 15, 135–53.

Linklater, Andrew (1992), 'What is a Good International Citizen?', in Paul Keal (ed.), *Ethics and Foreign Policy*, Canberra, Allen and Unwin, 21–43.

Linklater, Andrew (1998), *The Transformation of Political Community*, Cambridge, Polity.

Loth, Wilfred (1988), *The Division of the World – 1941–45*, London, Routledge.

Luban, David (1980), 'The Romance of the Nation-State', *Philosophy and Public Affairs*, 9:4, 392–7.

Lummis, C. Douglas (1991), 'Development Against Democracy', *Alternatives*, Vol. 16, 31–66.

Mahbubani, Kishore (1992), 'The West and the Rest', *The National Interest*, Summer, 3–12.

Mandani, Mahmood, Thanadika Mkandwire and E. Mamba-din-Wamba (1993), 'Social Movements and Democracy in the South', in Possna Wignaraja (ed.), *New Social Movements in the South*, London, Zed.

Marcuse, Herbert (1969), 'Repressive Tolerance', in R.P. Wolff, Barrington Moore and Herbert Marcuse (eds), *A Critique of Tolerance*, Boston, Beacon Press, 81–123.

Marks, Stephen (1998), 'From the "Single Confused Page" to the "Decalogue for Six Billion Persons": The Roots of the Universal Declaration of Human Rights in the French Revolution', *Human Rights Quarterly*, 20:3, 449–514.

Marx, Karl (1994), *Early Political Writings*, Joseph O'Malley (ed.), Cambridge, Cambridge University Press.

Mauzy, Diane K. (1997), 'The Human Rights and "Asian Values" Debate in Southwest Asia: Trying to Clarify the Key Issues', *Pacific Review*, 10:2, 201–36.

McCorquodale, Robert and Richard Fairbrother (1999), 'Globalization and Human Rights', *Human Rights Quarterly*, 21:3, 735–66.

McDonald, Laura (1999), 'Trade with a Female Face', in Annie Taylor and Caroline Thomas (eds), *Global Trade and Global Social Issues*, London, Routledge.

McGrew, A. (1992), 'A Global Society?', in S. Hall, D. Held and T. McGrew (eds), *Modernity and Its Futures*, Cambridge, Polity Press.

Meiksins Wood, Ellen (1995), *Democracy Against Capitalism*, Cambridge, Cambridge University Press.

Mittelman, James H. (1995), *Globalization: Critical Reflections*, Boulder, Lynne Rienner.

Mittelman, James H. (1996), 'The Dynamics of Globalization', in James H. Mittelman (ed.), *Globalisation: Critical Reflections*, Boulder, Lynne Rienner, 1–19.

Mittelman, James H. (1997), 'Restructuring the Global division of Labour: Old Theories and New Realities', in Stephen Gill (ed.), *Globalization, Democratization and Multiculturalism*, Basingstoke, Macmillan, 77–103.

Moskovitz, Moses (1974), *International Concern with Human Rights*, Dobbs Ferry, NY, Oceana Publications.

Mosler, Hermon (1980), *International Society as a Legal Community*, Netherlands, Sijthoff Noordhoff.

Muravchik, Joshua (1986), *The Uncertain Crusade: Jimmy Carter and the Dilemma of Human Rights Policy*, London, Hamilton Press.

Muzaffar, Chandra (1995), 'From human rights to human dignity', *Bulletin of Concerned Asian Scholars*, 27:4, 6–8.

Nardin, Terry (1983), *Law, Morality and the Relations of States*, Princeton, Princeton University Press.

Nossal, K.M (1998), 'Pinchpenny Diplomacy – The Decline of "good international citizenship" in Canadian Foreign Policy', *International Journal*, 54:1, 88–105.

Opsahl, T. (1989) 'Instruments of Implementation of Human Rights', *Human Rights Law Journal*, 10:1, 13–33.

Panitch, Leo (1995), 'Rethinking the Role of the State', in James Mittelman (ed.), *Globalization: Critical Reflections*, Boulder, Lynne Rienner.

Pasha, Mustapha Kamal and David L. Blaney (1998), 'Elusive Paradise: The Promise and Peril of Global Civil Society', *Alternatives*, 23:1, 417–50.

Peterson, V. Spike and Laura Parisi (1998), 'Are Women Human? It's Not an Academic Question', in Tony Evans (ed.), *Human Rights Fifty Years On: A Reappraisal*, Manchester, Manchester University Press, 132–60.

Plant, Raymond (1993), 'The Justification for Intervention: Needs Before Contexts', in Ian Forbes and Mark Hoffman (eds), *Political Theory, International Relations and the Ethics of Intervention*, Basingstoke, Macmillan.

Pugh, Mike (2000), 'The Social-Civil Dimension', in Michael Pugh (ed.), *Regeneration of War-torn Societies*, Basingstoke, Macmillan.

Ramphal, Sir Shridath (1992), 'Globalism and Meaningful Peace: A New World Order Rooted in International Community', *Security Dialogue*, 32:3.

Raphael, D.D. (1967), 'Human Rights Old and New', in D.D. Raphael (ed.), *Political Theory and the Rights of Man*, London, Macmillan, 54–67.

Robinson, A.H. and J.G. Merrills (eds) (1992), *Human Rights in the World*, Manchester, Manchester University Press.

Robinson, Fiona (1998), 'The limits of a rights-based approach to international ethics', in Tony Evans (ed.), *Human Rights Fifty Years On: A Reappraisal*, Manchester, Manchester University Press.

Robinson, G. (1997), 'Britain's Blind Eye to Inhumanity', *The Times*, 8 May, 20.

Robinson, M. (1993), 'Will Political Conditionality Work?', *IDS Bulletin*, 21:1, 58–66.

Robinson, William (1996), *Promoting Polyarchy: Globalization, US Intervention and Hegemony*, Cambridge, Cambridge University Press.

Roosevelt, Franklin D. (1941), Annual Message to Congress, 6 January.

Ropke, Inge (1991), 'Trade, development and sustainability: A critical assessment of the "free trade dogma"', *Environmental Economics*, Vol. 9, 13–23.

Rorty, Richard (1993), 'Human Rights, Rationality, and Sentimentality', in Stephen Shute and Susan Hurley (eds), *On Human Rights: Oxford Amnesty Lectures 1993*, New York, Basic Books.

Ruggie, John G. (1983), Human Rights and the Future of International Society', *Daedalus*, 112:4, 93–110.

Rupert, Mark (1997), *Producing Hegemony: The Politics of Mass Production and American Global Power*, Cambridge, Cambridge University Press.

Sakamoto, Y. (1991), 'The Global Context of Democratization', *Alternatives*, Vol. 16, 119–27.

Salih, M.A. Mohamed (1998), 'Globalization and Insecurity in Africa', paper given at the International Studies Association annual conference, February 1998.

Salmi, J. (1993), *Violence and the Democratic State*, Oxford, Oxford University Press.

Sanders, D. (1991), 'Collective Rights', *Human Rights Quarterly*, 13:3, 368–86.

Schachter, Oscar (1970), 'The Obligation to Implement the Covenant in Domestic Law', in *The International Bill of Rights: The Covenant on Civil and Political Rights*, Columbia, Columbia University Press.

Scholte, Jan Art (1996), 'Towards a Critical Theory of Globalization', in Eleonore Kofman and Gillian Youngs (eds), *Globalization in Theory and Practice*, London, Pinter, 43–57.

Sethi, Harsh (1997), 'Survival and Democracy: Ecological Struggles in India', in Ponna Wignerajo (ed.), *New Social Movements in the South*, London, Zed Books, 122–48.

Shivji, Issa (1999), 'Constructing a New Rights Regime: Promises, Problems and Prospects', *Social and Legal Studies*, 8:2, 253–76.

Shue, Henry (1980), *Basic Rights: Subsistence, Affluence and US Foreign Policy*, Princeton, Princeton University Press.

Sieghart, Paul (1983), 'Economic Development, Human Rights and the Omelette Thesis', *Development Policy Review*, Vol. 1, 95–104.

Singh, Someshwar (2000), 'Human Rights – A Charade of the Virtuous?', *Third World Resurgence*, No. 116, 40–1.

Spybey, Tony (1996), *Globalization and World Society*, Cambridge, Polity Press.

Stammers, Neil (1993), 'Human rights and power', *Political Studies*, vol. XLI, 70–82.

Stammers, Neil (1995), 'A critique of social approaches to human rights', *Human Rights Quarterly*, 17:3, 499–508.

Stammers, Neil (1999), 'Social Movements and the Social Construction of Human Rights', *Human Rights Quarterly*, 21:4, 980–1008.

Stein, A.A. (1982), 'Coordination and Collaboration: Regimes in an Anarchic World', *International Organization*, 36:2, 299–324.

Strong, Tracy (1980), 'Taking The Rank With What Is Ours: American Political Thought, Foreign Policy and the Question of Rights', in P.R. Newman (ed.), *The Politics of Human Rights*, London, New York University Press.

Summers, Lawrence H. (2000), Testimony to House Committee on Banking and Finance, 1 May.

Tamilmoran, V.T. (1992), *Human Rights in Third World Perspective*, New Delhi, Har-Anand Publications.

Tananbaum, Duane (1988), *The Bricker Amendment Controversy: A Test of Eisenhower's Political Leadership*, Ithaca, Cornell University Press.

Tang, James T.H. (1995), 'Human Rights in the Asia-Pacific Region: Competing Perspectives, International Discord and the Way Ahead', in James T.H. Tang (ed.), *Human Rights and International Relations in the Asia-Pacific*, London, Pinter, 1–9.

Tatum, J.S. (1996), 'Technology and liberty: Enriching the Conversation', *Technology in Society*, 18:1, 44–59.

Taylor, Annie (1997), 'NGOs and International Institutions: The Trade and Environment Debate', paper presented to the International Studies Association, Toronto, March 18–27.

Taylor, Annie (1998), 'The Significance of Non-Governmental Organisations in the Development of International Environmental Policy: The Case of Trade and Environment', unpublished PhD thesis, Department of Politics, University of Southampton.

Taylor, Annie (2001), 'Lost in Global Society: NGOs in the Trade and Environment Debate', forthcoming.

Taylor, Annie and Caroline Thomas (eds) (1999), *Global Trade and Global Social Issues*, London, Routledge.

Taylor, Lance and Ute Pieper (undated), *Reconciling Economic Reform and Sustainable Development: Social Consequences of Neo-Liberalism*, New York, UNDP.

Teśon, Fernando R. (1992), 'The Kantian Theory of International Law', *Colombia Law Review*, 92:1, 53–102.

Tetrault, M.A. (1988), 'Regimes and liberal world order', *Alternatives*, Vol. 13, 5–26.

Thomas, Caroline (1998), 'International Financial Institutions and Social and Economic Rights: An exploration', in Tony Evans (ed.), *Human Rights Fifty Years On: A Reappraisal*, Manchester, Manchester University Press, 161–85.

Tomasevski, Katerina (1989), *Development Aid and Human Rights*, London, Pinter Publishers.

Tomasevski, Katerina (1993), *Development Aid and Human Rights Revisited*, London, Pinter Publishers.

Tully, James (1995), *Strange Simplicity: Constitutionalism in an Age of Diversity*, Cambridge, Cambridge University Press.

UN Statistical Yearbook (1948), New York, United Nations.

UNDP (1994), *Human Development Report*, Oxford, Oxford University Press.

UNDP (1996), *Human Development Report*, Oxford, Oxford University Press.

UNDP (1997), *Human Development Report*, Oxford, Oxford University Press.

UNDP (1998), *Human Development Report*, Oxford, Oxford University Press.

UNDP (1999), *Human Development Report*, Oxford, Oxford University Press.

UNPO (Unrepresentative Nations and Peoples Organization) (2000), <www.unpo.org/member/ogoni/ogoni.html>.

UNRISD (United Nations Research Institute for Social Development) (1995), *States of Disarray: The Social Effects of Globalization*, London, UNRISD.

van de Pijl, Kees (1997), 'Transnational Class Formation and State Forms', in Stephen Gill and James Mittelman (eds), *Innovations and Transformations in International Studies*, Cambridge, Cambridge University Press, 105–33.

van der Pijl, Kees (1998), *Transnational Classes and International Relations*, London, Routledge.

Vincent, R.J. (1986), *Human Rights and International Relations*, Cambridge, Cambridge University Press.

Walker, R.B.J. (1990), 'Security, Sovereignty, and the Challenge of World Order', *Alternatives*, Vol. 15, 3–27.

Wallerstein, Immanuel (1983), *Historical Capitalism*, London, Verso.

Walzer, M. (1995), *Spheres of Justice: A Defence of Pluralism and Equality*, Oxford, Blackwell.

Waters, Malcolm (1995), *Globalization*, London, Routledge.

Watkins, Kevin (1996), *The Oxfam Poverty Report*, Oxford, Oxfam.

Watson J.S. (1976), 'A Realistic Jurisprudence of International Law', *Yearbook of International Affairs*, Vol. 30, 265–85.

Watson, J.S. (1979) 'Legal Theory, Efficacy and Validity in the Development of Human Rights Norms in International Law', *University of Illinois Law Forum*, Vol. 3, 609–41.

Weiss, Peter (1994), 'The Human Rights of the Underclass', in J. Cavanagh, D. Wysham and M. Arrunda (eds), *Beyond Bretton Woods*, London, Pluto Press, 29–38.

Wheeler, N. and Tim Dunne (1998), 'Good International Citizenship: A Third Way For British Foreign Policy', *International Affairs*, 74:4, 847–71.

Wight, Martin (1966), 'Why Is There No International Theory?', in H. Butterfield and M. Wight (eds), *Diplomatic Investigations*, London, George Allen and Unwin, 17–34.

Wilson, Richard A. (1997), 'Human Rights, Culture and Context: An Introduction', in *Human Rights, Culture and Context*, London, Pluto Press, 1–27.

Woodiwiss, Anthony (1998), *Globalization, Human Rights and Labour Law in Pacific Asia*, Cambridge, Cambridge University Press.

Woods, Ngaire (1999), 'Order, Globalization and Inequality in World Politics', in Andrew Hurrell and Ngaire Woods (eds), *Inequality, Globalization and World Politics*, Oxford, Oxford University Press, 8–35.

Young, Oran (1989), 'The Politics of International Regime Formation', *International Organization*, 43:3, 349–75.

Index